Home How-To
Handbook
Electrical

RICK PETERS

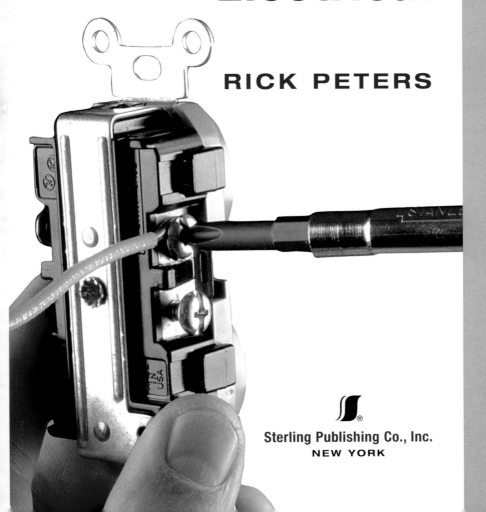

Sterling Publishing Co., Inc.
NEW YORK

Book Design: Richard Oriolo
Photography: Christopher J. Vendetta
Page Layout: Sandy Freeman
Contributing Editor: Cheryl Romano
Copy Editor: Barbara McIntosh Webb
Indexer: Nan Badgett

Library of Congress Cataloging-in-Publication Data Available

10 9 8 7 6 5 4 3 2 1

Published by Sterling Publishing Co., Inc.
387 Park Avenue South, New York, NY 10016

Distributed in Canada by Sterling Publishing
c/o Canadian Manda Group, 165 Dufferin Street,
Toronto, Ontario, Canada M6K 3H6
Distributed in the United Kingdom by GMC Distribution Services,
Castle Place, 166 High Street, Lewes, East Sussex, England BN7 1XU
Distributed in Australia by Capricorn Link (Australia) Pty. Ltd.
P.O. Box 704, Windsor, NSW 2756, Australia

Sterling ISBN 13: 978-1-4027-3200-3
         ISBN 10: 1-4027-3200-7

For information about custom editions, special sales, premium and
corporate purchases, please contact Sterling Special Sales
Department at 800-805-5489 or specialsales@sterlingpub.com

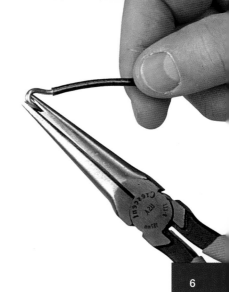

Contents

How to Use This Book   4

1 Electrical Basics   6

2 Materials   20

3 Tools   48

4 Electrical Know-How   58

5 Lighting Projects   98

6 Heating and Cooling Projects   134

7 Home Electronics   156

8 Adding and Extending Circuits   168

9 Troubleshooting Electrical Circuits   188

Index   206

Introduction

WE CAN'T SEE IT, touch it, or smell it, but the awesome power of electricity serves us every day. It cooks our food, heats and cleans our homes, and lights our way in the dark—usually so well that we take it for granted.

When something goes wrong, though, or we want to make a change, we usually call in an electrician. For some jobs, this is still the best and smartest route. But with more and more do-it-yourself-friendly products and tools available, plus some basic understanding, you can do a lot of the work yourself. That's what this book is all about—helping to demystify electricity so you can tackle a variety of electrical projects and repairs.

How to Use This Book

There are roughly three sections: basics, projects, and troubleshooting. The first section (chapters 1 to 4) starts with Electrical Basics. We take you from how electricity works to how power is generated and gets to your home. In Materials we guide you through the vast array of electrical materials, parts, and products on the market. Tools explores the everyday and specialty tools you'll need for working on your electrical system. In Electrical Know-How, you'll find the nuts and bolts of working with electricity: wire and cable, making solid connections, working with boxes, running cable, and installing switches and receptacles.

The second section, on projects (chapters 5 to 8), illuminates Lighting: how to install just about every kind of light fixture you'd want in your home. Then there's Heating and Cooling, including ceiling fans, bathroom exhaust fans, and programmable thermostats. Home Electronics is your "on" button for telephone, cable TV, and computer systems. In Adding and Extending Circuits, you'll find three different ways to get electricity to a new area of your home. The final section is Troubleshooting, where we share a systematic approach to tracking down and solving electrical problems.

Codes and Permits

If any of your projects involve adding, extending, or modifying circuits, check with your local building inspector for permit and inspection requirements. Typically, an inspector will check your work at the "rough-in" stage (no wall coverings in place) and again when all the finish work is done (receptacles and switches installed, etc.). By making sure your work is done to code, an inspector helps protect both your family and your home.

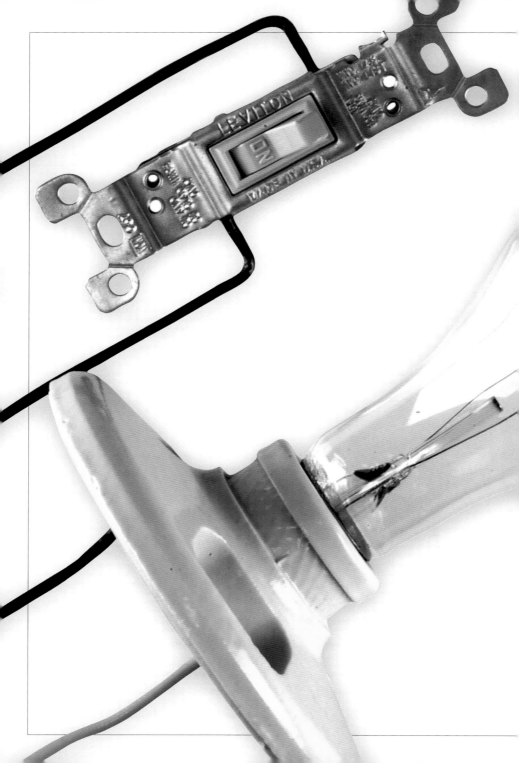

1

Electrical Basics

FLIP A SWITCH AND THERE IT IS: the electricity that powers our lives. This power demands respect, though, so before you tackle any electrical project, you need to understand how electricity works: how it flows from a power station to and through your home. In this chapter, we'll look at basic circuits and power distribution, plus safety issues like grounding, protecting, and defining your electrical system.

How Electricity Works

At its simplest, an electrical circuit consists of a power source, a control, and a load (such as a lamp); see the drawing below. These parts are connected with wires. With the switch open, no current flows and the light is off. Closing the switch completes a path for current, and the lamp lights up. Current (measured in amperes) flows from the power source (battery) through the switch and the load, and you get light. Electrical circuits are often shown as schematic diagrams, like the one here. (For more on electrical symbols, see page 17.)

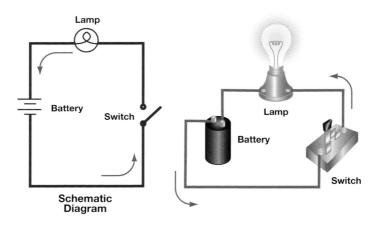

Direct versus alternating current

Current can be direct (DC) or alternating (AC). With direct current, the voltage, or electrical pressure that forces current to flow, stays steady over time; a car battery produces 12 volts to force current to flow in one direction only. With AC, the voltage constantly changes and periodically reverses in direction (top drawing on page 9). Your home is powered with alternating current because AC can be distributed over long distances with little loss of power (more on this on page 10).

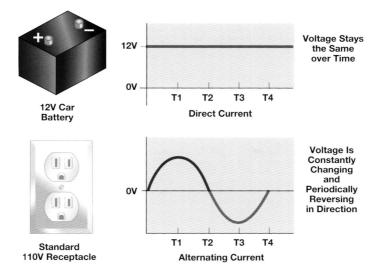

12V Car Battery

12V

0V

| T1 | T2 | T3 | T4 |

Direct Current

Voltage Stays the Same over Time

Standard 110V Receptacle

0V

| T1 | T2 | T3 | T4 |

Alternating Current

Voltage Is Constantly Changing and Periodically Reversing in Direction

Series and parallel circuits

All circuits are one of two types: series or parallel. In a series circuit, current flows through each part of the circuit in turn (drawing below). So if any element goes bad (a lamp burns out), current stops and the other loads are without power; old-fashioned holiday lights were wired in series. On a parallel circuit, current has separate paths for each load; if one goes bad, the others still work. The receptacles in your home are parallel-wired so that if one conks out, the others keep going.

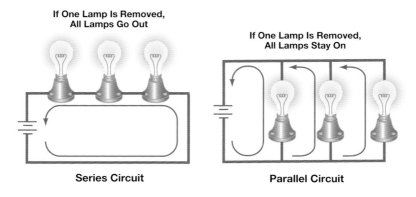

If One Lamp Is Removed, All Lamps Go Out

If One Lamp Is Removed, All Lamps Stay On

Series Circuit

Parallel Circuit

Power Distribution

Why is your home powered with alternating current? Mostly because of power distribution. It all starts at a power plant, where some form of energy is converted into electricity. Water, wind, or steam is harnessed to turn giant turbines to create alternating current. This current is fed to step-up transformers (drawing below) that dramatically boost the voltage (upwards of 500,000 volts) via large magnetic coils. This higher voltage lets the current easily travel long distances. High-voltage lines transfer the electricity to a substation, where the voltage is stepped down (reduced usually to 480 volts) and fed to local power lines. One more step-down transformer then lowers the voltage to the 240-volt lines that enter your home through the service mast, power meter, and service panel.

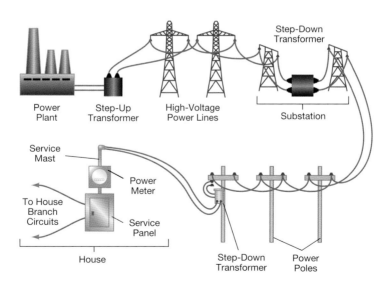

The service panel

New homes have three lines entering the service panel: two 120-volt lines ("hot" lines) and a grounded neutral line. Older homes have two lines: one 120-volt hot line and a grounded neutral. Inside the service panel, the neutral line terminates at the neutral bus bar (a bus bar is a metal strip that allows multiple connections). The two 120-volt lines connect to the main breaker and travel down along a hot bus bar on each side of the breaker (drawing below). Here, circuit breakers or fuses can be added to tap into the power so it can flow to a branch circuit (see page 12 for more on branch circuits). A ground spike provides an uninterrupted path for excess current to flow to ground (for more on grounding, see page 14).

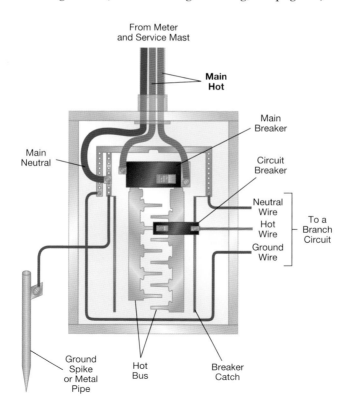

From Meter and Service Mast

Main Hot

Main Breaker

Main Neutral

Circuit Breaker

Neutral Wire

Hot Wire

Ground Wire

To a Branch Circuit

Ground Spike or Metal Pipe

Hot Bus

Breaker Catch

Branch Circuits

Your service panel is the heart of your home's electricity. From here (via fuses or breakers), current flows around your home through branch circuits. How the branches are connected depends on how your house was initially wired. Branches usually consist of logical groupings centered around rooms or functions (drawing below). A single breaker or fuse may protect all of the receptacles (or outlets) in a living room or bedroom; another might serve all the light fixtures in part of the home. Appliances often have their own dedicated breakers. Power-hungry units like electric dryers, ranges, cooktops, and wall ovens are typically protected by separate 240-volt, 40- or 60-amp fuses or breakers. The only way to tell at a glance which fuse or breaker controls which device in your home is to map your circuits (see pages 16–19).

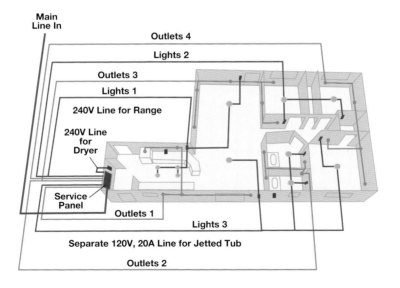

Main Line In
Outlets 4
Lights 2
Outlets 3
Lights 1
240V Line for Range
240V Line for Dryer
Service Panel
Outlets 1
Lights 3
Separate 120V, 20A Line for Jetted Tub
Outlets 2

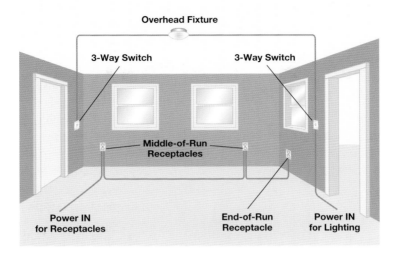

Overhead Fixture

3-Way Switch

3-Way Switch

Middle-of-Run Receptacles

Power IN for Receptacles

End-of-Run Receptacle

Power IN for Lighting

Typical room wiring

How the branch circuits in your home are wired depends mostly on your home's construction. In homes built on concrete slabs, the wiring commonly runs through the attic space and down the walls. In homes with basements or crawl spaces, wiring usually runs under the floor and then up the walls, as well as over-head (drawing above). In most modern homes, non-metallic cable (see page 24) is used throughout to connect the various receptacles, switches, and fixtures. Non-metallic cable typically houses three wires: a black or "hot" wire, a white "neutral" wire, and a bare copper or green "ground" wire. Current travels out of the fuse or breaker through the hot wire and returns on the neutral wire. For safety, the ground wire provides a continuous path back to ground (via the ground spike described on page 11) for excess current to flow through.

Grounding

Like any powerful force, electrical current can help or hurt. How it helps: Current in your branch circuits should flow in a complete loop, as long as the circuit is grounded and no faults, or "shorts," occur. How it hurts: Whenever current in a branch flows back to its fuse or breaker through a path other than the neutral wire, you get a ground fault.

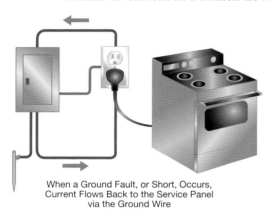

When a Ground Fault, or Short, Occurs, Current Flows Back to the Service Panel via the Ground Wire

When a ground fault or short occurs on a properly grounded circuit, potentially dangerous current will flow back to the circuit panel via the ground wire, and the breaker or fuse will trip. This "de-energizes" the circuit (drawing above left). If a ground fault occurs on an ungrounded circuit, the current has no return path, so the breaker won't trip. Here's the hurting part—a person could become that return path when he accidentally touches the ungrounded device and completes the circuit. The result: a nasty shock.

Grounding and polarization

For a ground system to work properly (and that means safely), your receptacles must

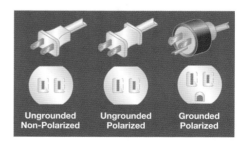

Ungrounded Non-Polarized Ungrounded Polarized Grounded Polarized

be grounded. Any device you plug in must also be grounded. Grounded receptacles are easy to identify by their third hole (bottom drawing on page 14). In addition to being grounded, your receptacles should also be polarized. Polarized receptacles ensure that current flows in the right direction through the connected device. The short slot is hot and the long slot is neutral.

GFCIs

GFCI stands for "ground-fault circuit interrupter"; it's a safety device that turns off power when a ground fault occurs. An electronic device inside called a comparator constantly monitors the current flowing in and out of the circuit. During

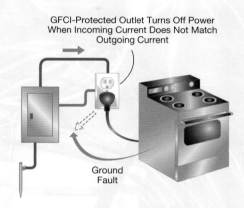

GFCI-Protected Outlet Turns Off Power When Incoming Current Does Not Match Outgoing Current

Ground Fault

normal operation, the current flowing into a circuit should be the same as the current flowing out. If they're not the same, some of the current is flowing where it should not. This can occur when an appliance or device is faulty, or when an accident happens, like dropping a plugged-in hair dryer into a sink full of water. If the circuit is GFCI-protected, power will shut off almost instantaneously (drawing above).

GFCI RECEPTACLES AND BREAKERS. GFCIs come in two basic flavors: receptacles and breakers. A GFCI receptacle can protect any device plugged into that receptacle, as well as other receptacles that are wired "forward" to the end of the circuit (for more on GFCI receptacles, see pages 88–89). GFCI breakers can protect an entire room such as a bathroom or kitchen (installing a GFCI breaker is best left to a licensed electrician).

Mapping Your Circuits

One day your washing machine dies and you suspect a fuse or breaker. How do you know which one is the culprit? You could test every single one, or you could just refer to your circuit map. This invaluable piece of paper attaches inside your service panel (photo at right) to let you identify your numbered breakers at a glance (drawing below). Besides making it easier to secure power to a room or device so you can work on it, it lets you know which fuse or breaker controls the different devices in your home, which can save a life in an emergency.

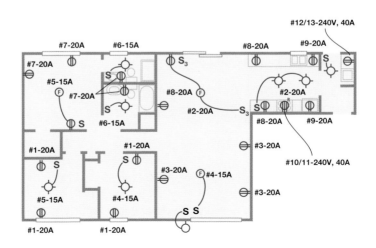

Electrical symbols

To properly map your circuits, you'll need to become familiar with some of the basic symbols used in electrical schematics, as shown below.

Common Electrical Symbols

Ceiling Light	Night-light
Wall Light	Indoor Telephone
Ceiling Ligting Outlet	Outdoor Telephone
Duplex Convenience Outlet	Push Button
Switch Convenience Outlet	Doorbell
Weatherproof Outlet	Door Buzzer
Electric Range	Radio Outlet
Electric Clothes Dryer	Television Outlet
Split-Wired Duplex Outlet	S Single-Pole Switch
Electric Motor	S₂ Double-Pole Switch
240-Volt Polarized Outlet	S₃ 3-Way Switch
Special-Purpose Outlet	S₄ 4-Way Switch
Ceiling Fan	Sₚ Switch with Pilot Light
Wall Fan	Swp Weathrproof Switch
Ceiling Junction Box	Electric Door Opener
Wall Junction Box	Service or Entrance Panel
Ceiling Pull Switch	Chimes
Clock Outlet	S Switch Wiring
Thermostat	Fluorescent Ceiling Fixture
Generator	Fluorescent Wall Fixture

1 SKETCH YOUR FLOOR PLAN. To map your circuits, start by drawing a rough sketch of the floor plan of your home—one for each floor, as illustrated in the drawing above. If you have access to your home's original blueprints, use these.

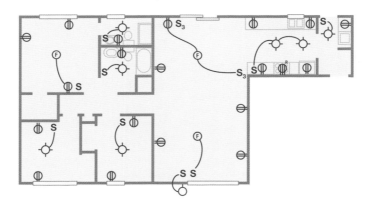

2 LABEL THE FIXTURES. Next, using the electrical symbols shown on page 17, note where each switch, receptacle, fixture, and appliance is on the drawing, as shown in the illustration above. Include windows, doors, and stairs for reference.

3 NUMBER CIRCUITS AT PANEL. Now go to the main service panel and place a numbered label on each breaker or fuse. Once you have determined which breaker or fuse controls which devices, write these numbers on the floor plan that you drew earlier.

4 TEST AND MAP THE FIXTURES. With the breakers labeled, first turn off all the breakers, or unscrew all the fuses; leave the main breaker on, or the main fuse in. Now flip one circuit breaker, or screw in one fuse at a time. Go through the house,

turning on switches and lights and checking the receptacles for power. Place a sticker on each powered device and note the breaker or fuse number (as indicated on the fuse or breaker) on the sticker (photo at left). After you've turned on each breaker or fuse and have checked the entire house for power, make sure every device is labeled. Then note these numbers on your map (along with their respective amperage ratings) and attach the map to the service panel or a nearby wall.

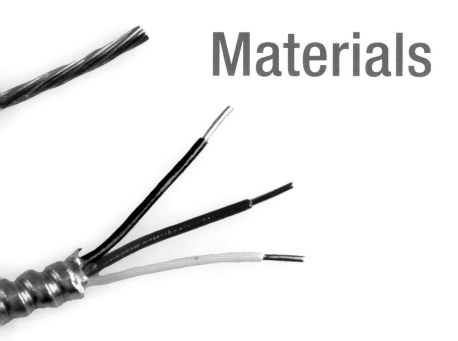

2

Materials

SOMETIMES IT'S HARD TO FEEL like a smart consumer—especially in the electrical aisles of home centers and hardware stores. Just to buy some plain old wiring for a project, you have to know a lot: how many conductors? What wire gauge? What type of shielding? This chapter is all about helping you to feel and be smart, so you can navigate those aisles and buy with confidence.

Wire and Cable

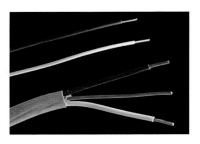

Wire and cable are not the same thing. Wires are individual conductors of electricity. Cable is two or more wires sheathed in a plastic or metal jacket (photo above). Most of the electrical devices in your home—receptacles, switches, fixtures, and appliances—are connected by cable (usually non-metallic; see page 24). In older homes, hollow tubes called conduit (see pages 32–33) were run from device to device, and individual wires were pulled through the conduit to connect the devices.

WIRE TYPES. Individual wires or conductors can be insulated or non-insulated; they can be a single solid conductor or a group of stranded, smaller wires, as shown in the photo at left. The bigger a conductor is, the tougher it is to bend; so large conductors are stranded to make them more flexible. Insulated wires carry current, and are color-coded as described in the chart below. Non-insulated (or "bare") wires are used mainly for grounding.

Wire Color Chart

WIRE COLOR	WHITE	BLACK	RED
FUNCTION	A neutral wire or "return" that conducts current at zero voltage.	A "hot" wire that conducts current at full voltage.	A "hot" wire for switching that conducts current at full voltage.

WIRE COLOR	WHITE WITH BLACK MARKINGS	GREEN	BARE COPPER
FUNCTION	A "hot" wire for switching that conducts current at full voltage.	An insulated conductor that serves as a path for grounding.	A bare conductor that serves as a path for grounding.

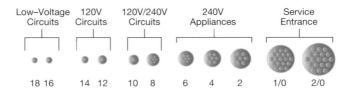

Low–Voltage Circuits	120V Circuits	120V/240V Circuits	240V Appliances	Service Entrance
18 16	14 12	10 8	6 4 2	1/0 2/0

WIRE GAUGE.

Wire is sized according to the American Wire Gauge (AWG) system; see the chart at right. The smaller the gauge, the larger the wire, as shown in the drawing above. You'll use 12- and 14-gauge wire the most in your home electrical projects.

Wire Gauge, Capacity, and Use

WIRE GAUGE	CAPACITY	TYPICAL USE
2/0	175 amps	Service
1/0	150 amps	entrance
2	100 amps	Electric furnace,
4	80 amps	central air
6	60 amps	conditioning
8	45 amps	Cooktop, wall
10	30 amps	oven, clothes dryer, window air conditioner
12	20 amps	Receptacles,
14	15 amps	switches, light fixtures
16	13 amps	Extension cords,
18	10 amps	low-voltage lighting, lamp cords

ALUMINUM WIRE AND CABLE

Before the 1970s, aluminum wire instead of copper was used in some homes. But aluminum wiring was found to be a safety hazard—as it expands and contracts over time, it can work loose from connections. If your home is wired with aluminum, call in a licensed electrician to make sure it's installed properly and is safe to use.

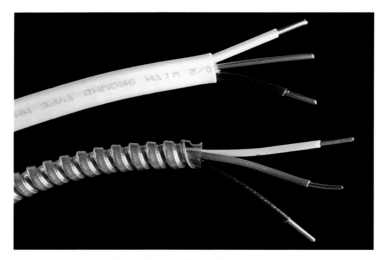

CABLE TYPES. The cable you'll use for your electrical projects will be either non-metallic (NM) or metallic, depending on the job. Non-metallic cable is commonly run throughout your home where it's basically protected—by either wall, ceiling, or floor coverings. Metallic cable is used to connect devices that may need to move or are exposed and unprotected. The sheathing of NM cable is plastic; the sheathing of metallic cable is flexible metal (usually aluminum).

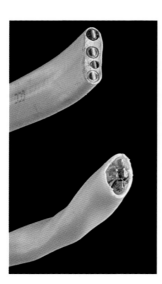

EXTERIOR-RATED CABLE. Similar to ordinary NM cable is exterior-rated cable—often called underground cable or UF (underground feeder). The big difference is that the conductors in UF cable are encased in thermoplastic. Compare the top exterior-rated cable in the top in the photo at left with the standard NM indoor cable shown beneath it. Because the conductors are encased, underground cable can be buried directly in the ground (check your local code for trench size, location, depth, etc.).

When you're ready to buy cable for a project, you'll need to identify a sheathing type (NM or metallic), how many conductors in the cable, and the wire gauge of the conductors.

NUMBER OF CONDUCTORS. The most common cable types are 2-wire and 3-wire (photo at right). No, the photo isn't wrong: The number of conductors in a cable can be misleading. This is because there are actually three wires in a 2-wire cable and four wires in a 3-wire cable. A 2-wire cable has a black "hot" wire, a white neutral wire, and a bare copper wire—the ground wire doesn't get counted. Likewise, a 3-wire cable has a black and white wire along with a red "control," and a bare copper ground. Typically 3-wire cables are used for wiring switches to light fixtures; 2-wire is used for most everything else.

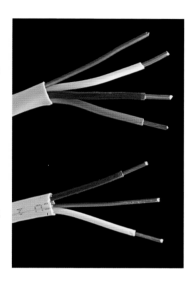

GAUGE OF CONDUCTORS. Finally, you'll need to specify the gauge of the conductors in the cable. The gauge you use will depend on the current in the branch. Most branch lines in your home will be either 15- or 20-amp—that's 14-gauge and 12-gauge conductors, respectively. If in doubt, check the fuse or breaker for the branch. Then match your wire gauge to its amperage rating (chart on page 23). For example, a 20-amp breaker requires 12-gauge conductors.

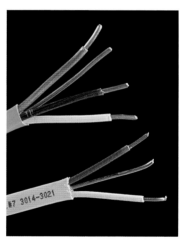

Electrical Boxes

For everyone's safety, the National Electrical Code requires that all circuit connections be made in an approved electrical box. This means that every time you splice wire together or connect wire to a device like a switch, the connection must be made in a box. There are many styles and types of boxes to choose from (photo at right). The box you choose for a project will depend on how many conductors it needs to hold (see the chart below), along with what will be installed in the box (switch, receptacle, etc.). Boxes come in three basic shapes: rectangular, square, and octagonal. Rectangular boxes house a switch or receptacle. Square boxes can hold pairs of switches or receptacles; octagonal boxes are used mainly for ceiling-mounted fixtures.

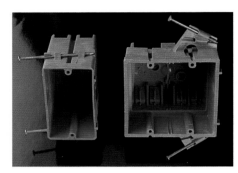

Number of Conductors Per Box

	14-GAUGE CONDUCTORS	12-GAUGE CONDUCTORS	10-GAUGE CONDUCTORS
4" square, 1½" deep	10	9	8
4" square, 2⅛" deep	15	13	12
4" octagonal, 1½" deep	7	6	6
4" octagonal, 2⅛" deep	10	9	8
3×2 rectangular, 1½" deep	3	3	3
3×2 rectangular, 2¼" deep	5	4	4
3×2 rectangular, 3½" deep	9	8	7

New-construction boxes

So how do you pick an electrical box for a project? First, determine whether the box will be used for new

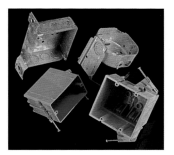

construction or old construction (remodel work). New-construction boxes are used when studs are exposed. Old-construction boxes, often called "cut-in" boxes, can be used with the wall covering in place (see page 28).

New-construction boxes are made of metal or plastic. They're easy to identify, since they either have a nailing flange or will house nails set at an angle to the box, as shown in the photo at left. Most boxes have built-in brackets, flanges, or fastening systems that require no additional fasteners. Just grab a hammer and go.

(see page 28).

Gangable Boxes

Some metal electrical boxes can be joined or "ganged" together. Pros often carry this type of box for its flexibility: Its metal side plates can be removed to join together two or more single boxes to create any width box needed.

MATERIALS

Old-construction boxes

Like new-construction boxes, old-construction or remodel boxes come in many shapes, sizes, and materials. All old-construction boxes have a built-in clamp or clamps to secure the box to the wall covering—they don't need to be attached to a stud or ceiling joist. This means that you can "cut in" a remodel box just about anywhere you want.

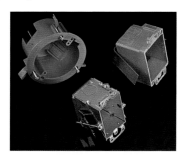

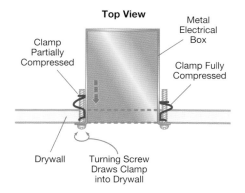

Top View

Clamp Partially Compressed

Metal Electrical Box

Clamp Fully Compressed

Drywall

Turning Screw Draws Clamp into Drywall

METAL REMODEL BOX. The clamps for a metal remodel box are on the side of the box. With the box in place, screws on each side are tightened to compress the clamps and grip the wall covering.

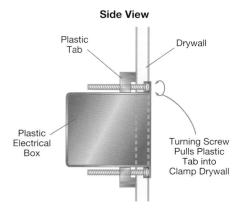

Side View

Plastic Tab

Drywall

Plastic Electrical Box

Turning Screw Pulls Plastic Tab into Clamp Drywall

PLASTIC REMODEL BOX. On a plastic remodel box, clamps are on the top and bottom of the box. Turning the screws on the clamps—basically plastic tabs—pulls the tab into the wall covering to grip it.

CABLE CLAMPS. Since electrical boxes house cables, every box must be able to clamp the cable(s) in place to prevent connections from pulling apart. Metal boxes have built-in or add-on clamps (drawing below). Plastic boxes have built-in flexible tabs that are forced open to feed the cable(s) into the box, as shown.

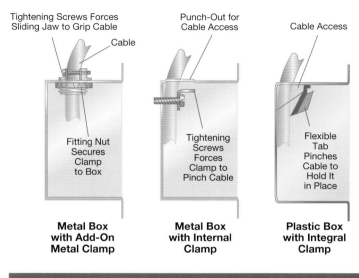

Tightening Screws Forces
Sliding Jaw to Grip Cable

Cable

Punch-Out for
Cable Access

Cable Access

Fitting Nut
Secures
Clamp
to Box

Tightening
Screws
Forces
Clamp to
Pinch Cable

Flexible
Tab
Pinches
Cable to
Hold It
in Place

**Metal Box
with Add-On
Metal Clamp**

**Metal Box
with Internal
Clamp**

**Plastic Box
with Integral
Clamp**

QUICK FIX

Box Extenders

When you attach a wall covering to an existing wall— like ceramic tile over drywall—you'll discover that the added thickness makes it tough to reinstall cover plates. The solution is to extend a switch or receptacle out so it ends up flush with the new wall, using a box extender. These come in different sizes to handle varying wall thickness. Some are backless boxes; other are plastic tabs (green strips in the photo) that slip between the switch or receptacle and the box.

Specialty boxes

There are three common types of specialty boxes used for electrical projects: ceiling boxes, pancake boxes, and weatherproof boxes.

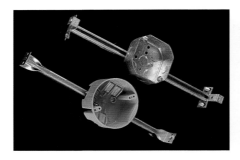

CEILING BOXES. The type of ceiling box you use will depend on what it has to support. Plastic boxes are for light-weight fixtures only. Use metal boxes and brackets for heavy fixtures (photo above). Ceiling fans require a special box rated to support their weight (see pages 136–143).

PANCAKE BOXES. A pancake box is designed for installations where wall or ceiling thickness is a problem. They're often used for ceiling fixtures, and are secured directly to the bottom of a ceiling joist (top right photo). Since the shallowness of a pancake decreases the number of conductors the box can hold, check your local code to see whether these boxes are approved for use in your area.

WEATHERPROOF BOXES. Electrical boxes designed for out-door installation are weatherproof (middle photo). A foam-rubber gasket is often sandwiched between the box and the cover plate to create a weather-tight seal.

Connectors

Focus on connectors as your connection to staying safe (especially if you find the chart below less than exciting). The wires inside electrical boxes are usually connected with either screw-on wire nuts or crimped metal compression sleeves.

WIRE NUTS. Wire nuts connect wires quickly, and they're color-coded so you'll know how many wires you can safely splice together; see the chart below. Quality wire nuts contain a square-cut spring inside. This cuts into and grips the wires as the nut is twisted into place. For more on using wire nuts, see page 64.

COMPRESSION SLEEVES. Metal compression sleeves look sort of like bullet casings with the bottom cut off (middle photo). They're used mostly to join bare copper ground wires together in a box. The ends of the wires are inserted into the sleeve, and the sleeve is compressed or crimped with a special tool (see page 50) to lock the wires in place. A plastic-jacketed version of this is also available for joining together insulated wires, or anytime you just want the added protection of insulation.

Wire Nut Capacities

COLOR	CAPACITY
Red	#18 to #10 AWG Min. 2 #14 Max. 2 #10 w/ 2 #12
Yellow	#18 to #12 AWG Min. 2 #18 Max. 4 #14 w/ 1 #18
Orange	#22 to #14 AWG Min. 1 #18 w/ 1 #20 Max. 4 #16 w/ 1 #20
Blue	#22 to #14 AWG Min. 2 #22 Max. 3 #16
Gray	#22 to #16 AWG Min. 2 #22 Max. 2 #16

Conduit

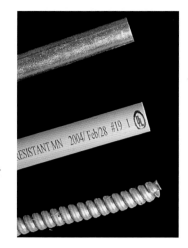

Before non-metallic (NM) cable was allowed by code, the wires that connected fixtures and devices in older homes were housed in metal or plastic conduit. Conduit is simply a hollow pipe, either metal or plastic. Although much more expensive and time-consuming to install, conduit offers a couple of advantages over NM cable. Conduit, particularly metal conduit, protects wires much better than the thin plastic sheathing of NM cable. Also, if the wiring goes bad in conduit, you just pull it out and use fish tape (page 52) to run new wires—*without* removing wall coverings, as you'd need to do with NM cable.

Wiring that will be exposed (such as in a basement or garage with masonry walls) must be protected with conduit: either metal conduit (often called EMT), plastic conduit (PVC), or flexible conduit (see the photo above). Technically, flexible conduit is actually armor-clad cable, but it's referred to as flexible conduit anyway. Regardless of the type of conduit you're using, each size has a set number of conductors it can hold; see the chart at left.

Maximum Wires Allowed in Conduit

TYPE AND SIZE OF CONDUIT	14-GAUGE WIRES	12-GAUGE WIRES	10-GAUGE WIRES
1/2" EMT	12	9	5
1/2" PVC	10	7	4
3/4" EMT	22	16	10
3/4" PVC	18	13	8
1" EMT	35	26	16
1" PVC	32	23	15
1 1/2" EMT	84	61	38
1 1/2" PVC	80	58	36

METAL CONDUIT. Metal conduit comes in a variety of diameters, with ¾" the most common. Although metal conduit can be cut with a hacksaw, bending it takes special tools (see page 52). To make metal conduit easier to work with, a variety of shaped fittings are available (bottom left photo).

PLASTIC CONDUIT. Plastic conduit, fittings, and boxes are gaining popularity, as they're inexpensive, non-conductive, and easy to work with (middle photo). Plastic conduit cuts easily with a handsaw or miter saw, and is joined together with PVC cement just like plumbing fittings (see page 97). As with metal conduit, the fitting types are many and varied. On the downside, the thicker walls of plastic conduit mean it holds fewer conductors than the same diameter in metal (see the chart on page 32).

FLEXIBLE CONDUIT. Since flexible conduit is, well, flexible, special fittings aren't needed for the bends. All you really need are transition fittings to connect the cable to electrical boxes. The two most common types are screw-in and slip-on, as shown in the bottom right photo.

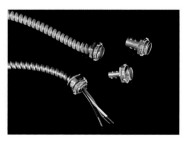

Switches

Switches are everyday, kind of ho-hum items...unless we don't have them to control things like lights, garbage disposals, and vents. Then, they become special and important. For your electrical projects, you'll work mostly with single-pole and 3-way switches; specialty switches (pages 36–37) are also common.

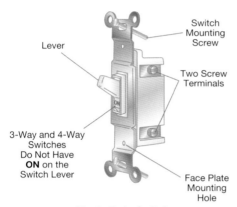

Lever

Switch Mounting Screw

Two Screw Terminals

3-Way and 4-Way Switches Do Not Have **ON** on the Switch Lever

Face Plate Mounting Hole

Single-Pole Switch

SINGLE-POLE. A single-pole switch is the most common in a home. It controls a fixture or receptacle from one location. It's easy to identify, as it has only two screw terminals on one side (not counting a ground lug). And the lever of the switch has clearly labeled ON and OFF positions. (See pages 78–80 for wiring details.)

3-WAY. A 3-way switch controls a light fixture or receptacle from two locations. You can tell these apart from single-pole switches in two ways. First, you'll find three screw terminals instead of two: Two like-colored screws are called "travelers," and the darker (or black) terminal is the common screw. Second, since these switches can be up or down for on or off, the lever has no markings. (See pages 81–82 for wiring details.)

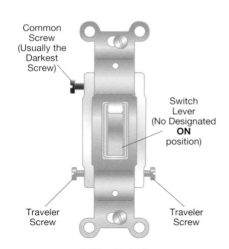

Common Screw (Usually the Darkest Screw)

Switch Lever (No Designated **ON** position)

Traveler Screw

Traveler Screw

3-Way Switch

4-WAY. Because they control a light fixture or receptacle from three or more locations, 4-way switches are not very common. If your home has large rooms or long hallways, you may find a 4-way version helpful. As with single-pole and 3-way switches, you can tell a 4-way switch by the number of screw terminals: It has four—two pairs of "travelers." A 4-way switch is always installed between a pair of 3-way switches (see page 83 for wiring details).

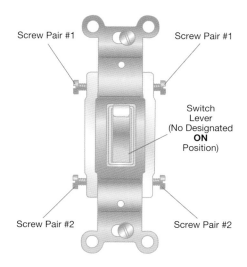

4-Way Switch

SWITCH STYLES. Once you know which type of switch you need (single-pole, 3-way, etc.), you start the tough work: choosing among all the decorative options available. You'll have decisions to make on color (typically white,

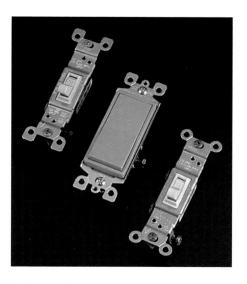

almond, and gray), plus the lever style: standard and paddle (photo above). Hands old and young appreciate the ease of use that paddle-style switches offer over the much smaller levers on standard switches.

Specialty switches

Want to get fancy? There are specialty switches to suit any need, including varieties called pilot, timer, double, dimmer, and motion-activated.

Pilot light switches have a built-in indicator that lights when power flows through the switch and the fixture. These are especially useful for controlling devices that you can't readily see—like exhaust fans and garage lights. Note: This type of switch requires a neutral wire, so don't use it to replace a single-pole switch, where there are only two hot wires in the box.

A timer switch allows a fixture or appliance to run for a specified time before turning it off automatically. This type of switch is most often used to control a vent in a bathroom or kitchen. Turn the knob to the desired setting and the fan turns off after the set time has elapsed.

A double switch controls two fixtures or receptacles from a single location. On most installations, both switches are powered by the same circuit—

one wire (called the feed wire) is connected to both halves of the switch; then two separate wires run power to the individual fixtures.

A dimmer switch lets you vary the brightness of a lighting fixture. You can find them in a wide variety of styles: slide action, lever type, and the most common, the dial type. You can replace any standard single-pole switch with a dimmer switch; but 3-way dimmers are also manufactured to replace a standard 3-way switch.

A motion-activated switch employs the same technology as security motion detectors: An infrared beam is projected out over an area. When the beam is interrupted, the switch turns power on to a fixture or other device. After a pre-set time, it switches power off (if no further motion is detected).

P R O T I P

Grades of Switches

★ Like any other home improvement material, you get what you pay for in electrical switches. You'll find two "grades" available at your local home center: standard and commercial (sometimes called "pro" grade). A commercial-grade switch has a stouter body, and it's made of higher-quality materials. It does cost more, but wouldn't you rather install a switch that you know will last longer and hold up better over time? We thought so.

Receptacles

What most of us call outlets are technically receptacles. By any name, they provide convenient access to branch circuits in a variety of voltages and amperages. Receptacles may be grounded or ungrounded. Voltage options include 120 or 240 volts. And amperage ratings for receptacles in the average home range from 15 amps all the way up to 60 amps. The most common receptacles you'll find in your home will be 120-volt, 15- and 20-amp duplex receptacles.

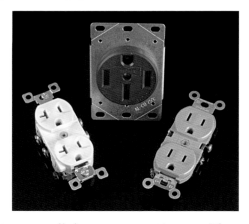

GROUNDED RECEPTACLES. Electrical code now requires that all receptacles in a home be grounded. How can you tell whether yours are? It's all in the face. What you're looking for is the telltale third prong hole below the two standard slots (right receptacle in the photo below). If you have do have old-style, two-slot receptacles in your home (left receptacle in photo below), you can't just

replace them with grounded receptacles. If you do this without creating means for grounding, the circuit will be unsafe. One approved solution is to replace them with GFCI receptacles (see page 15). Because safety is such a concern here, you should consult with a licensed electrician before doing any work.

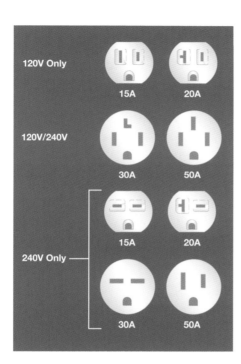

120V Only — 15A, 20A

120V/240V — 30A, 50A

240V Only — 15A, 20A, 30A, 50A

AMPERAGE AND VOLTAGE RATINGS. Although many receptacles look similar, you can distinguish among them by examining the type and number of slots on the face. These slots identify the voltage and current that the receptacle can handle. When you replace a receptacle, you should exchange it with an identical part. Check the back of the receptacle for both a voltage and current rating, or take it with you to the home center or hardware store.

Receptacle Grades

Just as with electrical switches (pages 34–37), you'll usually find two grades of receptacles: standard and commercial. Note the heavy-duty construction and thicker body of the commercial-grade receptacle (on the right in the photo) compared to the standard receptacle. Higher-quality materials combined with thicker, more rigid parts make for long-lasting, problem-free products. If you can, invest in these beefier, better-made receptacles for your next electrical project.

Breakers and Fuses

Your home's electrical system has watchdogs that never sleep or eat, and are on the job 24/7: These are circuit breakers or fuses. They constantly monitor current flow throughout the various branch circuits, and can shut down a circuit instantly if they detect too much current. Not only does this protect your wiring from overheating, but it also protects your entire home from possible fire. Circuit breakers have replaced fuses (page 42) as the primary way of protecting from over-current in today's homes. Their big advantage is that they can be reset once they've "tripped"; fuses must be replaced.

BREAKER BRANDS. With most electrical parts, the brand is unimportant. That is, single-pole switches made by two different companies are basically interchangeable; this isn't true with breakers. Breakers are brand-specific—they're designed to fit in only one brand of service panel. So, to buy a new or replacement breaker, you need to know the maker. Both of the breakers in the middle photo are rated to protect a 120-volt, 20-amp circuit. But notice how different the attachment system is for each; obviously, these are not interchangeable; take the breaker with you when buying a replacement.

BREAKERS' RATINGS. Circuit breakers are rated to handle 120-, 240-, or both 120- and 240-volt circuits, and to provide current protection ranging from 15 to 200 amps. Single-pole circuit breakers (left breaker in bottom photo) control current for loads that use only one leg of the 240 volts available in most breaker panels. Double-pole circuit breakers (right breaker in photo) control the current on loads that use both legs of the 240 volts available in a panel.

Breaker manufacturers sell a variety of types and sizes, along with specialty units that can be found in many homes. The two most common specialty breakers are split and GFCI breakers.

SPLIT BREAKERS. Split breakers provide two-for-one spacing in a crowded service panel. Say you want to add a 15-amp branch circuit and there are no more empty slots in your service panel. Simply replace an existing 15-amp breaker with a 15-amp split breaker (photo at left), and you're on your way (for more on adding circuits, see pages 182–187).

GFCI BREAKERS. A ground-fault circuit interrupter (GFCI) breaker is typically used to protect a branch circuit going to a kitchen or bathroom, where water can pose potential hazards. A GFCI breaker (bottom photo) monitors and compares the current flowing in and out of the branch circuit. If they're not the same, some of the current is flowing where it should not—and a ground fault or short occurs. When this happens, the CFCI breaker trips immediately, shutting off power to the entire branch.

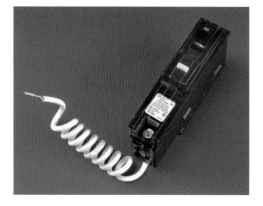

MATERIALS

Fuses are safety devices that "blow" when they detect a current overload. In older homes, the two types of fuses you'll deal with most often are cartridge and plug fuses.

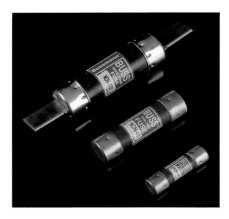

CARTRIDGE FUSES. Cartridge fuses usually protect 240-volt circuits. Ferrule-type cartridge fuses protect circuits up to 60 amps. Knife-blade cartridge fuses, identified by a metal blade at each end of the fuse, can handle circuits above 60 amps, up to a high range of around 600 amps. Always remove and replace a cartridge fuse with a fuse puller (see page 52)—and make sure to use an exact replacement fuse.

PLUG FUSES. There are three basic types of plug fuses: standard, time-delay, and tamper-proof. Standard fuses blow almost the instant that current exceeds their designated limit. Time-delay fuses can withstand a momentary surge of current, as when an appliance starts up. The problem with both standard and time-delay fuses is that they all have the same size threads. This lets you unscrew a 15-amp fuse and replace it with a 30-amp fuse—always a bad idea. To prevent this, type-S or tamper-proof fuses and adapters were developed. They have smaller plastic threads and are designed to fit only the correct-current-rated adapter.

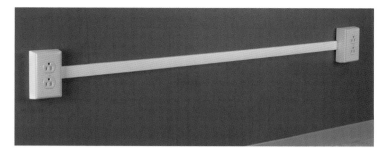

Surface-Mounted Wiring

Want another receptacle or light fixture in a room, but don't want the cost and effort of cutting into your walls? Consider surface-mounted wiring. Surface-mounted wiring (also known as on-wall wiring) allows you to tap into an existing branch line and extend it without having to call in an electrician. Surface-mounted wiring runs on the surface of the wall instead of inside the wall. Yes, it is more noticeable, but it's a lot less intrusive. (For more on installing surface-mounted wiring, see pages 170–175).

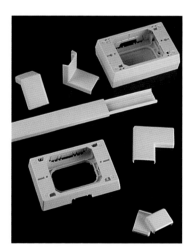

SURFACE-MOUNTED SYSTEM COMPONENTS. The heart of surface-mounted wiring is a hollow channel called "raceway." It comes in standard 5-foot lengths and has a cover that snaps over the channel to conceal the wiring. Various boxes include a "starter" box that lets you convert an existing box to handle the raceway, and deep, extra-deep, and two-gang boxes for mounting switches, receptacles, and fixtures. Corners and junctions are handled by inside, outside, and flat elbows, along with T-fittings.

Service and Sub-Panels

Your service panel is like an air traffic controller for electricity. The panel directs power to various points in your home and constantly monitors its progress, just as a controller directs a plane to a specific runway and then watches it land and taxi to a gate. Once the plane arrives at the gate, control is turned over to the ground crew. In your service panel, control is handed over to a fuse or breaker that monitors a single branch circuit. Busy airports often have smaller, separate control centers for smaller aircraft. Even though they still oversee traffic, control is passed along to the smaller control center. A sub-panel or switch box is used in much the same way — it protects branch circuits away from the main service panel.

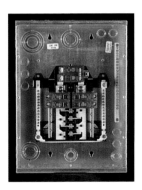

SERVICE PANELS. Modern service panels (photo at left) can handle anywhere from 100 up to 800 amps; 200-amp panels are the most common in new homes. Each panel holds a set number of breakers. A main service panel will have a main breaker, a hot bus that runs down the center of the panel, and a neutral/grounding bus located on opposite sides of the hot bus.

SUB-PANELS. Sub-panels are used where multiple branches need to run a distance from the main panel — such as for a new addition to the home. The advantage here is that you need to run just a single cable to the sub-panel and then branch out, instead of running multiple cables. If the distance is great, this can save a lot of money.

Light Fixtures

If you're replacing or upgrading a light fixture, you have lots of company: This is one of the most popular electrical projects. A new light fixture is a great way to quickly make over any room. You should get acquainted with the basic types of artificial lighting: general, task, accent, and decorative, whether standard or recessed.

General lighting illuminates a large area—think of an overhead fixture. Task lighting brightens a specific area, such as a countertop used for food preparation. Accent

lighting is any fixture that highlights an architectural or interior feature of a room. Decorative lighting is, well, purely decorative, and adds ambience or sets a mood.

GENERAL LIGHTING. General lighting (top photo) lets you move around your home safely. In days past, general lighting consisted of an incandescent or fluorescent overhead fixture. Today, the trend is toward recessed lighting (see page 47; see pages 100–103 for installation details).

TASK LIGHTING. Task lighting (like the under-cabinet light in the bottom photo) puts light where you need it to perform tasks like food preparation. Under-cabinet lighting comes in a variety of shapes and configurations, with strip lights and individual "pucks" the most common. When choosing under-cabinet lighting, go with halogen—it creates a more natural light than fluorescents, which tend to cast a greenish tint on surfaces. (See pages 120–123 for details on installing under-cabinet lighting.)

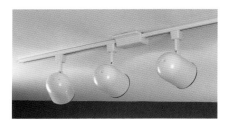

ACCENT LIGHTING. Accent lighting is designed to show off a feature in a room. Accent lighting can be as simple as enhancing a cabinet with interior lighting or adding track lighting to showcase wall art. Track lighting is one of the more popular forms of accent lighting, because individual lamps snap into a track anywhere along its length to spotlight different areas of the room or special wall treatments. (For details on installing track lighting, see pages 104–106.)

DECORATIVE LIGHTING. Decorative lights come in a huge variety zof styles and finishes. Wall sconces are commonly used for decorative purposes (middle photo); just realize that these are for setting a mood or highlighting an architectural feature and need to be supplemented with general lighting (see pages 108–113 for details on installing a wall sconce).

RECESSED LIGHTING. Recessed lights (commonly called "cans") are quickly replacing the single overhead fixtures in new homes, because they provide much better overall lighting. Also, since these lights are recessed, they're less intrusive and create a clutter-free ceiling. When you're shopping for recessed lights, keep things simple by buying a kit—these fixtures are widely sold in separate pieces (trim, can, etc.), and it takes a pro to play mix-and-match successfully. Also, these lights come in versions for new construction and for remodeling; for more on this, see pages 114–119.

IC and Non-IC Recessed Lamps

When selecting recessed lighting, make sure to choose the type that's rated for insulation contact. These lights can be installed in the ceiling without having to move the insulation out of the way (which would create an unwanted path for warm or cool air to leak out of your home).

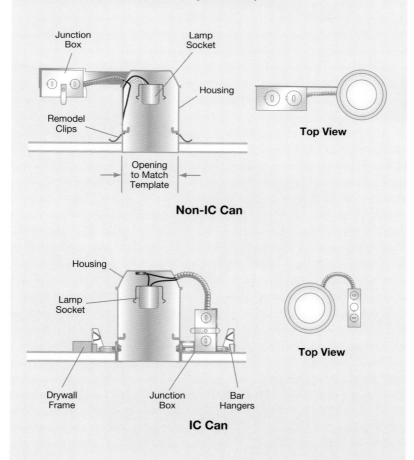

Junction Box

Lamp Socket

Housing

Remodel Clips

Top View

Opening to Match Template

Non-IC Can

Housing

Lamp Socket

Top View

Drywall Frame

Junction Box

Bar Hangers

IC Can

MATERIALS

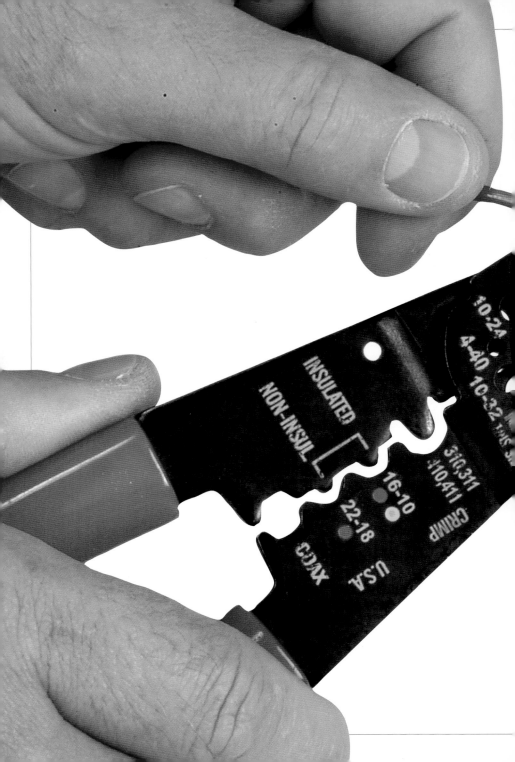

3

Tools

A CELLPHONE...AN EYELASH CURLER...a pair of wire strippers...according to Webster's, each is a tool: "a handheld device that aids in accomplishing a task." When your tasks are electrical, let this chapter take you through the most common "handheld devices" you'll need for your projects. We'll look at everything from general-purpose tools such as screwdrivers and electric drills to specialty tools like wire strippers, conduit benders, and circuit testers.

Wire and Cable Tools

Besides the basic hand tools most do-it-yourselfers have in their toolboxes (pages 54–55), the other tools you'll reach for most when tackling an electrical project are tools for working with wire and cable. These include wire strippers, combination stripper/crimpers, diagonal cutters, electrician's pliers, needle-nose pliers, and cable rippers.

WIRE STRIPPERS.
Wire strippers are pliers-like tools with notched and sharpened inner jaws that accept different wire gauges. You fit a wire in a notch, squeeze the handles to cut through the insulation, and pull out the wire.

COMBINATION TOOL.
A combination tool is a hybrid wire stripper and crimper. You use the crimping portion of the tool below the jaw pivot point to crimp on compression sleeves (page 31) and crimp-on connectors.

DIAGONAL CUTTERS.
Diagonal cutters sport a pair of sharpened jaws to cleanly cut wires in the 10- to 22-gauge range. Their tapered point allows you to access places that electrician's pliers (page 51) can't reach.

ELECTRICIAN'S PLIERS. Electrician's or linesman's pliers can cut larger-gauge wires than diagonal pliers can. They also feature square, serrated tips that let you grip, pull, and bend wire or cable.

NEEDLE-NOSE PLIERS. The serrated jaws of needle-nose pliers are tapered so you can reach into tight quarters. They're helpful when bending and twisting wire for making connections.

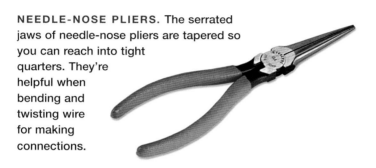

CABLE RIPPER. Although you can use a knife to cut the sheathing of non-metallic cable (page 24), it's easy to damage the wires inside. A better method is to use a cable ripper. Slide the ripper over the cable and squeeze it so the cutting point penetrates the sheathing; pull the cable through to rip it.

Specialty Tools

In some situations, you'll save time and aggravation by reaching for specialty tools. Three of the most useful for your electrical projects are a conduit bender, fish tape, and a fuse puller.

CONDUIT BENDER. If you're planning on working with rigid metal conduit (pages 32–33), you'll need a conduit bender for bending the conduit around corners. Although a conduit bender is easy to use, it takes practice to create accurate bends.

FISH TAPE. A fish tape (commonly called a "snake" in the trade) is the magic device that lets electricians pull wire through conduit and existing walls. It's a coil of flexible wire with a hook on one end housed in a plastic case. You "fish" the tape though a hole, attach a wire to it, and then pull the wire back through the hole.

FUSE PULLER

If you live in an older home that has cartridge-style fuses (page 42) in a service or sub-panel, you'll want to keep a pair of non-conducting fuse pullers on hand. Slip the appropriate-sized notched end over the body of the cartridge, squeeze, and pull out the fuse. The holder keeps your hands out of the circuit and prevents shocks.

Remodeling Tools

Power tools can make quick work of many tedious jobs. For your electrical remodeling jobs, you'll be especially grateful for two tools: a reciprocating saw and an electric drill.

RECIPROCATING SAW. If demolition work will be part of your electrical project, a reciprocating saw (often referred to by the brand name Sawzall) can quickly and aggressively cut through wall coverings and framing.

ELECTRIC DRILL. The two types of electric drill you'll find most useful for electrical work are a cordless drill and a right-angle drill. Because you often have power off where you're working, a battery-powered drill is a necessity. And since much electrical work is done in tight quarters (such as between wall studs), a right-angle drill will let you get in spaces a standard drill won't. Note how the drill chuck on a standard drill (right in photo) is in line with the motor, versus the chuck on a right-angle drill (left in photo), which is at 90 degrees to the motor.

Basic Hand Tools

Even the most barebones toolbox should include certain essentials. If yours doesn't already, be sure to stock it with these basic hand tools: screwdrivers, tape measure, level, utility knife, putty knife, stud finder, and drywall saw.

SCREWDRIVERS. Multi-tip screwdrivers (like the top screwdriver in the photo) pack a lot of punch in a small space. At minimum, you'll want a 4-in-1 that features two different-sized Phillips and slotted bits. Safety note: Never use a magnetized screwdriver for electrical work—the magnetic tip is easily attracted to metal and can cause an accidental short circuit.

LAYOUT TOOLS. Some of your projects will call for locating electrical boxes or fixtures. Two invaluable tools for this: an accurate tape measure and a small torpedo level.

INSULATED SCREWDRIVERS

If it makes you nervous to stick a metal screwdriver into an electrical box or fixture—don't. Instead, use an insulated screwdriver. It's designed just for working on electrical circuits; the body is a tough non-conducting plastic, and the only metal is the small tip on its end.

UTILITY AND PUTTY KNIVES.
For electrical work, you'll find a
utility knife handy to trim
cable sheathing,
fine-tune the fit of
a box in drywall,
etc. A putty knife
is useful for removing
old fixtures, baseboards,
and trim.

ELECTRONIC STUD FINDER. If any of
your electrical projects require that you cut
into a wall, you'll first need to locate the
wall studs. An electronic stud finder
is the tool for the job. Recent
advancements in
technology have
driven down their
price while jacking
up their accuracy.

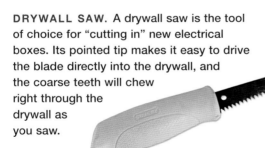

DRYWALL SAW. A drywall saw is the tool
of choice for "cutting in" new electrical
boxes. Its pointed tip makes it easy to drive
the blade directly into the drywall, and
the coarse teeth will chew
right through the
drywall as
you saw.

Testing Devices

Since electricity itself is invisible, you need special devices to test for its presence or absence. The most common testing devices for electrical work are circuit and continuity testers, receptacle analyzers, amp probes, and multi-meters (also called multi-testers).

CONTINUITY AND CIRCUIT TESTERS. The least expensive—and most limited—testers you can buy are continuity and circuit testers. A continuity tester does just one thing: It tests for continuity, a continuous unbroken path for current. These testers are nothing more than a battery, a lamp, and a pair of probes; if a path is continuous, the lamp lights when touched with both probes. A circuit tester sports two test leads (usually red and black) that are used to check for power. A bulb inside the tester lights in the presence of 120 volts. And that's all it does—it doesn't measure any other voltage, can't test for current or resistance.

RECEPTACLE ANALYZER. A plug-in receptacle analyzer reveals the condition of a receptacle's wiring. Just plug it in and it gives visual indicators of the receptacle's voltage, polarity, and grounding (for more on these, see page 191).

AMP PROBE. Normally, when you want to measure current in a branch circuit, you have to temporarily break the circuit and install the meter in series with the circuit (for more on this, see page 193). To get around this inconvenience, test equipment makers developed the amp probe. With this handy tool, you don't have to break the circuit. Instead, you pinch the cable or cord you want to measure between the retractable jaws of the probe. The digital or analog display will instantly give you an accurate current reading.

MULTI-METERS. Multi-meters or multi-testers come in digital and analog versions. Most folks find the digital versions much easier to use; the advanced electronics inside the meter let you touch the meter leads to a point and you get a digital read-out. (An analog meter can be quite difficult to read; see page 192 for an example of this.) The multi-meter shown in the photo below can accurately measure voltage (both AC and DC), current (in amps, both AC and DC), and resistance (measured in ohms). For more on using this invaluable diagnostic tool, see pages 192–193).

TOOLS

4

Electrical Know-How

SINCE EVERYTHING IS EASY when you know how, this is the chapter that makes your projects, well, at least easier. We'll look at essential skills, one technique at a time: how to prepare, join, and route wire and cable, work with electrical boxes, make connections, wire switches and receptacles, and occasionally work with conduit.

Working Safely with Electricity

Like any powerful force, electricity demands respect, or else: The potential for electrical shock is always present. If you religiously follow the safety guidelines here, you'll greatly reduce the chance of being shocked.

SECURE AND TAG POWER. Before you work on a circuit, secure the power. Once power is off, stick a piece of tape labeled NO! over the breaker or fuse (photo above). This simple step can prevent a potentially dangerous situation—you're working on a circuit when someone else in the house realizes they don't have power; they go to the panel and flip the breaker ON, energizing the circuit (and you).

INSULATE YOURSELF. If you need to work in or around a service panel or on an appliance or device that's encased in metal, you should insulate yourself from ground by wearing rubber-soled shoes and/or standing on a rubber mat (photo above). This is particularly important if the floor is wet or damp.

THE ONE-HAND RULE. At times, you'll probably need to work on an energized circuit: when replacing a breaker or adding or removing a line. Unless you've had the power temporarily disconnected by the power company, there'll still be power inside the panel— even if the main breaker is off. NEVER reach inside with both hands—if you do this, you complete a circuit and the current will flow directly through your heart. Keep one hand behind your back at all times, as shown in the photo at right.

120/240 Vac 1PH. 3W.
▲ 240 Vac 3PH. 3W.
MAIN LUGS ONLY

When used as service equipment, all unused neutral terminals may be used for terminating equipment ground wires.

▲ FOR GROUNDED "B" PHASE SYSTEMS, USE 240 Vac CIRCUIT BREAKERS ONLY. MAIN TERMINALS SUITABLE FOR NO. 8 TO NO. 1 WIRE.

Use only Square D type QO, QOA and class CTL QOT circuit breakers and replacement parts with this product.

Suitable for use with 75°C copper or aluminum main conductors.
See branch breakers for branch wire ratings.

(UL) **LISTED**
CLASS CTL
ENCLOSED PANELBOARD
ISSUE NO. C-2491

MADE IN MEXICO [73] 40269-901-07

USE ONLY UL-LISTED DEVICES. When you do go to replace a part, make sure it's UL-listed. UL stands for the Underwriters Laboratories, an organization that tests electrical devices for safety. UL parts have been tested and cleared for use in your home; check each part and look for the UL label (as shown in the photo above) before you buy it.

Preparing Wire

Every electrical project requires working with wire. The two most common tasks: removing insulation and cutting wire to length.

Removing insulation

The quickest, most reliable way to remove insulation from wire is to use wire strippers (page 50).

1 Start by matching the gauge of the wire you're working with to the corresponding notch in the stripper. Insert the wire and close the jaws (photo above).

2 Rotate the stripper roughly 180 degrees while holding the wire to prevent it from twisting. This cuts the insulation so you can pull the wire stripper to slide the cut insulation off the wire (right photo).

QUICK FIX

Repairing Insulation

If you remove too much insulation or accidentally nick the insulation, you can re-insulate the wire by slipping on a piece of heat-shrink tubing (photo at left). This handy tubing comes in various diameters and will shrink to fit snugly on the wire. The heat source? A standard hair dryer.

CUTTING STANDARD WIRE.
Wire in the 10- to 22-gauge range is easily cut with a pair of standard diagonal cutters (photo above). Don't cut anything heavier than 10-gauge with these—if you do, you run the risk of breaking the cutter or "springing" the jaws.

CUTTING HEAVY-GAUGE WIRE. The larger, beefier diagonal cutters shown above are capable of handling larger-gauge wires. When cutting heavy-gauge wire, position the wire as far down into the jaws as possible to concentrate the cutting force.

EYE PROTECTION

✚ It's common when preparing wire to remove a tad too much insulation and have to trim the solid conductor to length. Before you do this, put on protective eyewear. The tiny wire cut-offs, particularly on

heavier-gauge wire, are extremely dangerous. When you trim a conductor, the cut-off will fly off as if it were a bullet...a bullet with sharp edges. Protect your eyes from these dangerous bits of shrapnel, and make sure anyone else in the room wears eye protection.

Joining Wire

The most reliable way to join together two or more wires is to use a wire nut. Begin by stripping ½" to ¾" of insulation off each wire with wire strippers (page 62). Then select the correct-sized wire nut (page 31). Although you can use a wire nut without twisting the wires together, pros often do this as added insurance, especially if the connection will be exposed to vibration or repeated cycles of hot and cold (which can work the wires loose over time).

1 Grip the tips of the wires with a pair of electrician's pliers. Then, while holding the wires firmly in your other hand, twist the pliers to form a "pigtail" splice.

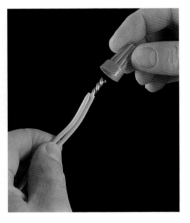

2 If necessary, trim the pigtail so that when the wire nut is screwed on, no bare copper is exposed. Turn the wire nut clockwise to tighten it, counterclockwise to loosen. Twist the nut until you meet firm resistance. Then gently pull each of the wires to make sure the connection is solid and that there's absolutely no chance that they'll come loose.

Using compression sleeves

Compression sleeves are commonly used to join together two or more bare ground wires.

1 With insulated wires, it's best to twist the ground wires together first before adding the compression sleeve.

2 Slip the compression sleeve over the twisted ground wires. Then use a crimper or a combination tool (page 50) to compress the sleeve onto the twisted wires.

PRO TIP

Pigtail Grounds

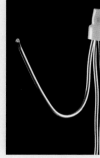

In middle-of-run switches and receptacles (pages 78–79 and page 84, respectively), multiple cables enter a single electrical box. This makes space inside the box limited. To minimize overcrowding, pros usually splice all of the grounds together along with a single ground line (called a pigtail ground), which is run to the ground lug of the switch or receptacle.

Preparing Cable

Because it's easy to work with, non-metallic (NM) cable is the most popular type for home wiring projects. The outer plastic sheathing is flexible, readily cut, and easily removed.

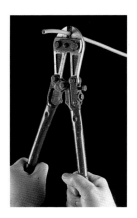

CUTTING NM CABLE. Although NM cable can be cut with a stout pair of diagonal cutters or electrican's pliers, a cable cutter or mini-bolt-cutter will do the job with least effort (photo at right).

Ripping NM cable

To use NM cable, you'll need to strip off the outer sheathing to expose the wires, cut the wires to length, and then strip the wire. To remove the outer sheathing, cut it down its length, peel it back, and then cut it away. A cable ripper is the tool for this job.

1 To use a cable ripper, position it about 8" from the end and squeeze it so the cutting point penetrates into the sheathing.

2 Now grip the cable ripper firmly in one hand while securely holding the cable in the other. Pull the cable ripper toward the cut end as you continue to squeeze the ends of the cable ripper together. After you've split the cable, peel back the outer sheathing and cut off the excess.

Routing Cable

If your project involves running new lines, there are two basic ways to rout cable to the new location: through the walls, and through the top or bottom plates.

To run cable along the length of a wall, you'll need to first drill access holes before pulling the cable.

1 DRILL THE ACCESS HOLES. Whenever you drill a hole in a stud for cable, use the smallest diameter possible and always drill the hole centered on the width of the stud. This gives the least weakening of the stud's load-bearing capacity.

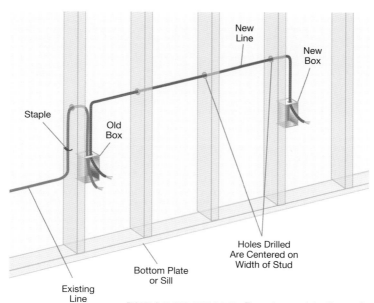

New Line

New Box

Staple

Old Box

Existing Line

Bottom Plate or Sill

Holes Drilled Are Centered on Width of Stud

THROUGH WALLS. Running cable through walls is most common in new construction, where the studs are exposed.

2 PULL THE CABLE.
Carefully thread the cable through the holes in the studs. For longer runs, a helper is useful to keep the cable from kinking as you pull.

THROUGH TOP OR BOTTOM PLATES. In remodel work, cable is typically routed through the top or bottom plates.

Double Top Plate

New Hole

Existing Hole

Existing Line

New Box

Old Box

Alternately, Cable Can Run Up through Bottom Plate

SECURING CABLES.
Once a cable is run into
an electrical box, it
needs to be secured
to the wall studs with
staples. This prevents
connections inside the
box from being pulled
apart if the cable is
accidentally pulled (say
by someone tripping
over a cable in an attic).

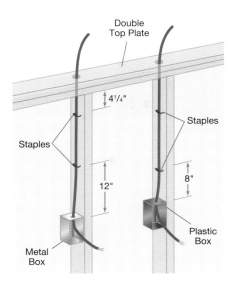

METAL FRAMING.
Some homes are
framed with metal
instead of wood studs.
Because it can be
difficult to drill through
these to run cable,
metal studs have
pre-punched holes
at regular intervals. To
protect the cable from

the sharp edges of the pre-punched holes, makers of metal studs
also sell easy-to-use snap-in insulators.

PROTECTIVE METAL PLATES

Whenever you run a cable
through a stud, always
apply a metal protective plate
over the cable. This will prevent
anyone from accidentally nailing
or screwing through the stud
and into the cable once the wall
covering is in place.

To route cable through a top or bottom plate of a wall, you'll first have to cut a hole in the wall covering. Then you can drill a hole through the plate and route the cable. A fish tape offers the most reliable, least frustrating way to route cable through studs, plates, and walls.

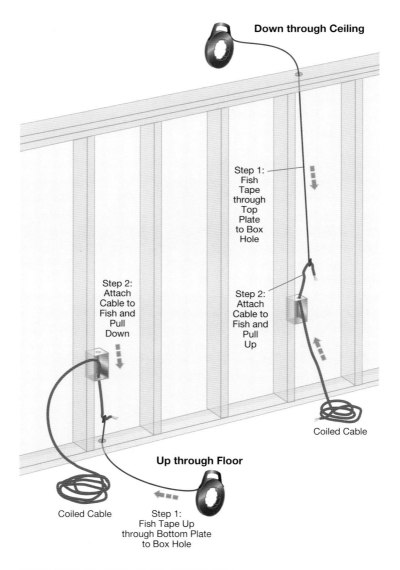

Down through Ceiling

Step 1: Fish Tape through Top Plate to Box Hole

Step 2: Attach Cable to Fish and Pull Down

Step 2: Attach Cable to Fish and Pull Up

Coiled Cable

Up through Floor

Coiled Cable

Step 1: Fish Tape Up through Bottom Plate to Box Hole

1 CUT ACCESS HOLE. Start by locating the studs with a stud finder. Use a drywall saw to cut a hole on the desired side of the stud. In most cases, a 3"-wide by 4"-tall hole will provide enough clearance to drill.

3 PREPARE THE CABLE. To attach a cable to a fish tape, remove 4" of sheathing. Then thread the conductors through the end of the tape about halfway and bend them back over themselves. Wrap electrical tape as smoothly as possible around the conductors and the end of the fish tape.

2 DRILL THROUGH PLATE. Because you'll be drilling at an angle, you'll need either a long drill bit or a bit extender to drill all the way through the plate. Use a ½"- to ¾"-diameter bit and hold the drill away from the wall covering to prevent damage.

4 PULL THE CABLE. The easiest way to pull cable with a fish tape is to have a helper pull on the tape as you feed the cable. Slow down near the taped joint so it doesn't catch on the rough edges of the plate hole.

Working with Boxes

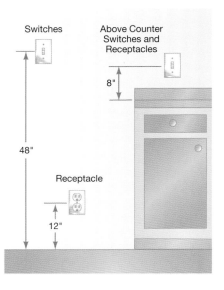

Switches

Above Counter Switches and Receptacles

8"

48"

Receptacle

12"

Electrical boxes protect electrical connections and make them accessible for future work; all boxes must be accessible (you can't bury one inside a wall). Where and how you mount a box will depend on whether it's new or old construction and on your local code. Although there are general guidelines for box locations (drawing above), it's best to check with your local building inspector for specifics.

New-construction boxes

Most new-construction boxes have a built-in gauge that lets you position the box on the studs so the box will end up flush with the finished wall. If a box doesn't have this, hold a piece of the finished wall material up against the stud and slide the box forward until it's flush.

BUILT-IN NAILS.
Hold the box in place and hammer in the nail to secure it to the stud.

SIDE FLANGE. Drive screws or nails through the side flange and into the stud.

If you mix metal electrical boxes with non-metallic cable, you must protect the cable from the jagged edges of the box's openings. If the cable isn't fastened to the box, it can move (due to vibration, house settling, etc.), damaging the sheathing and insulation. The result can be wires touching metal or other wires. The solution: internal or add-on clamps.

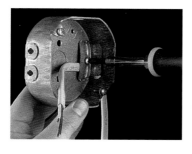

INTERNAL CLAMPS. Slip the cable between the clamp and the box and tighten it enough just to secure the cable; don't crush the wires.

Add-on clamps

Add-on clamps attach to a box with a locknut; the cable is secured to the connector with a pair of screws.

1 REMOVE KNOCK-OUT. Knock-outs are holes punched almost completely though a metal box. A small section is left attached to the box to hold it in place. To remove a knock-out, first tap it with a hammer or electrican's pliers to wedge it open. Then grasp the knock-out with pliers and twist.

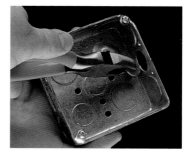

2 INSTALL CLAMP AND CABLE. Position the add-on clamp in the knock-out hole and thread on the locknut. Slip the cable through the clamp and tighten the cable clamp screws.

Installing a remodel box

Remodel or "cut-in" boxes are easy to install because you don't have to attach them to a stud—they have built-in clamps that grip the wall.

1 LOCATE THE BOX. Position your box away from any studs. Press it into the wall at the desired height and use a level to check for plumb; then trace around it.

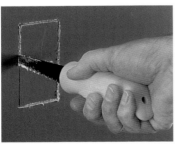

2 CUT THE HOLE. Push the tip of a drywall saw through the drywall at one corner and cut to the opposite corner; repeat for the other three sides.

3 INSTALL THE BOX. In most cases, you'll want to feed your cable up into the hole that you just cut and pass it through the box before inserting the box in the wall.

4 SECURE THE BOX.

Secure the box to the wall by tightening the built-in clamp screws. These screws will pull the box tight against the wall via plastic tabs on the top and bottom of the box, or metal clamps on the sides of the box.

PRO TIP

Box Straps

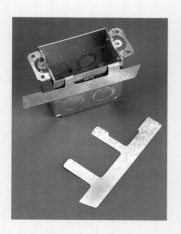

★ Any box that has drywall ears (the small L-shaped brackets on the top and bottom of a box) can be installed in an existing wall with a pair of metal box straps. You cut a hole in the wall and then insert the box. Then you slip a strap (one on each side of the box) between the box and the opening. While holding the box in place, you pull the strap forward as far as possible; then fold in the metal "arms" (as shown) to support the box.

Making Connections

The number one cause of electrical problems is poor connections: wires connected poorly to switches, receptacles, and fixtures, and wires improperly joined. That's why it's so important to master the skill of making flawless connections. For switches and receptacles, wires are attached via screw or push-in terminals. Wire-to-wire connections use wire nuts and compression sleeves (see pages 64–65).

Connecting to screw terminals

1 PREPARE THE WIRE. Strip ¾" of insulation off each wire with a wire stripper. Since you'll be bending this wire into a loop in the next step, it's especially important not to nick the wires. If you do by accident, trim the end of the wire off at the nick and re-strip the wire.

2 SHAPE THE WIRE. With a pair of needle-nose pliers, form a C-shaped loop on the end of the wire to wrap around the screw.

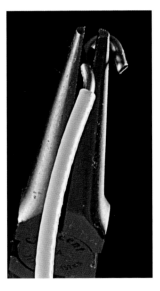

3 SECURE THE WIRE. Hook the wire around a screw terminal so that it forms a clockwise loop; this way as you tighten the screw, it will pull the loop tighter instead of forcing it open. Tighten the screw firmly and make sure that no insulation is captured under the head of the screw.

Connecting to push-in terminals

In addition to screws, some receptacles and switches are designed to accept a wire that's pushed into an opening in the back of the device. A spring inside firmly grips the wire and makes a quick electrical connection.

1 PREPARE THE WIRE. On the back of receptacles that accept push-in wiring, there's a gauge that indicates how much wire to strip. There's also an opening (rectangular slot below the wire hole) for releasing the wire.

2 PUSH IN TO CONNECT. Insert the stripped end into the correct opening. Push the wire firmly into the opening so that no bare copper is exposed. Then gently tug on the wire to make sure the spring is gripping it securely.

PRO TIP

Why Pros Don't Use Push-In Wiring

If you had X-ray vision, you could look inside a receptacle and see how push-in wiring works. As a wire is inserted, it forces a thin metal spring back to "capture" the wire. Compare this to a connection made by wrapping a wire around a tightened screw, and it's easy to see why the pros don't use push-ins: They're just not reliable.

Small Spring Makes Contact with Conductor

Release

Push-In Terminal

Single-Pole Switch Wiring

A single-pole switch controls the hot leg of a circuit—a hot wire is attached to each terminal. The color and number of wires in the box vary, depending on where the switch is located in the circuit.

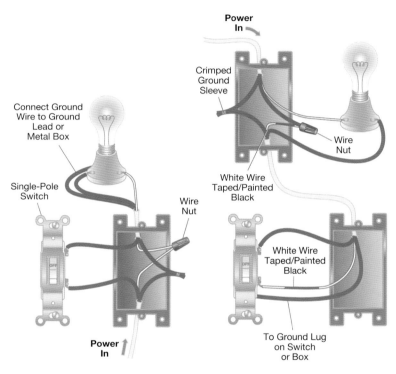

Power In

Crimped Ground Sleeve

Connect Ground Wire to Ground Lead or Metal Box

Wire Nut

Single-Pole Switch

Wire Nut

White Wire Taped/Painted Black

White Wire Taped/Painted Black

Power In

To Ground Lug on Switch or Box

POWER ENTERS SWITCH BOX. The simplest wiring setup for a single-pole switch is when power enters the switch box.

POWER ENTERS FIXTURE BOX. If only a single cable enters the box, then the switch is at the end of the run (often referred to as a switch loop). One of the hot wires is black, but the other hot wire is white; the white wire is wrapped with electrician's tape or painted black to indicate that it's hot.

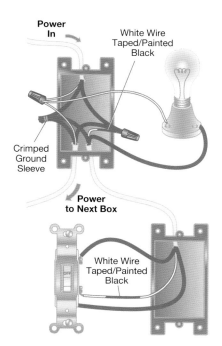

Power In

White Wire Taped/Painted Black

Crimped Ground Sleeve

Power to Next Box

White Wire Taped/Painted Black

SWITCH IN MIDDLE OF CIRCUIT. Having three cables entering the box signals that the switch is in the middle of the circuit, often called a "middle-of-run" switch.

TAPING THE WHITE/HOT LEAD

Frequently a white "neutral" wire is used as a "hot" wire when wiring switches. To make this clear to future electricians and homeowners, it's important to always mark the white wire as "hot" by wrapping it with black electrician's tape or painting it black.

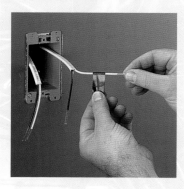

Here's how to wire a single-pole switch.

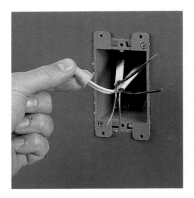

1 **SPLICE THE NEUTRALS TOGETHER.** Strip insulation off all white wires and use a wire nut to splice them together.

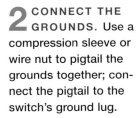

2 **CONNECT THE GROUNDS.** Use a compression sleeve or wire nut to pigtail the grounds together; connect the pigtail to the switch's ground lug.

3 **CONNECT THE HOT WIRES TO THE SWITCH.** Strip insulation off the hot wires, loop the ends with needle-nose pliers, and attach the wires to the screw terminals on the switch.

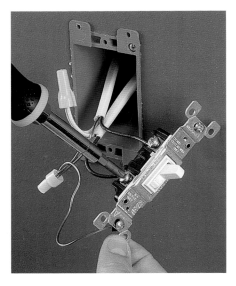

3-Way Switch Wiring

A 3-way switch has three screw terminals; to control power to a fixture from two separate sites, they're always installed in pairs. A 3-way switch requires a 3-wire system—typically 12/3 with ground or 14/3 with ground (see page 25), depending on the amount of current flowing through the cable. Of the three terminals on the switch, one has a distinctive color and is marked COM for common. This is the terminal that the hot or black wire connects to.

The other two terminals are for traveler wires that "travel" to the switches and inter-connect them. There are three wiring options for 3-way switches: Power enters the switch box (see drawing at right), power enters the fixture box, or power goes through both switches to the fixture (see the drawings on page 82).

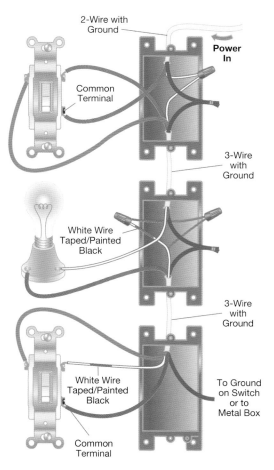

2-Wire with Ground

Power In

Common Terminal

3-Wire with Ground

White Wire Taped/Painted Black

3-Wire with Ground

White Wire Taped/Painted Black

To Ground on Switch or to Metal Box

Common Terminal

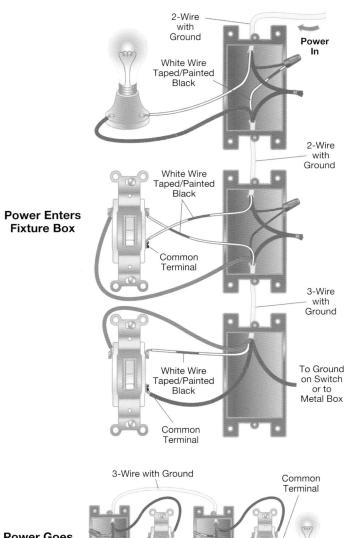

2-Wire
with
Ground

**Power
In**

White Wire
Taped/Painted
Black

2-Wire
with
Ground

White Wire
Taped/Painted
Black

**Power Enters
Fixture Box**

Common
Terminal

3-Wire
with
Ground

White Wire
Taped/Painted
Black

To Ground
on Switch
or to
Metal Box

Common
Terminal

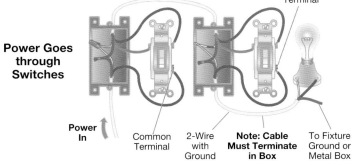

3-Wire with Ground

Common
Terminal

**Power Goes
through
Switches**

**Power
In**

Common
Terminal

2-Wire
with
Ground

**Note: Cable
Must Terminate
in Box**

To Fixture
Ground or
Metal Box

4-Way Switch Wiring

A 4-way switch is always installed between a pair of 3-way switches to control a set of lights from three or more locations.

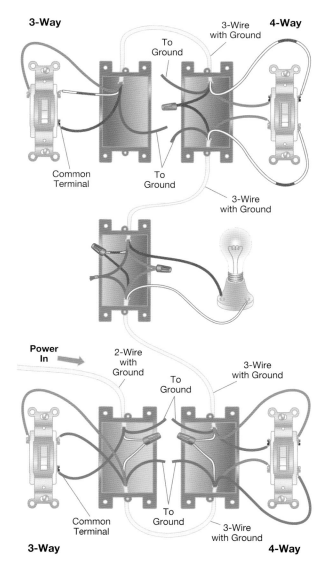

3-Way

3-Wire with Ground

4-Way

To Ground

Common Terminal

To Ground

3-Wire with Ground

Power In

2-Wire with Ground

To Ground

3-Wire with Ground

Common Terminal

To Ground

3-Wire with Ground

3-Way

4-Way

Receptacle Wiring

Household receptacles have two pairs of screw terminals on their sides. One pair is brass or black; the other pair is silver. Hot wires (black or red) are connected to the brass terminals; white wires are connected to the silver (neutral) screw terminals. Most also have a ground lug for connecting the ground wires. Receptacles may be wired at the end or middle of a "run" or circuit.

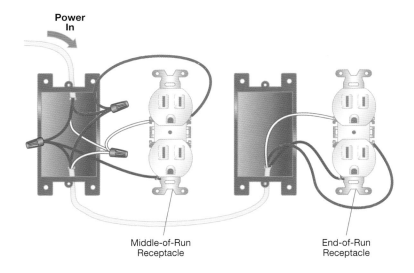

Power In

Middle-of-Run Receptacle

End-of-Run Receptacle

Switch-controlled receptacle

In most cases, receptacles in your home are constantly "live" or "hot"; that is, power is always available at the receptacle. In some situations, you may want to control the power via a switch. You can control both halves of the outlet or just one plug-in; see below.

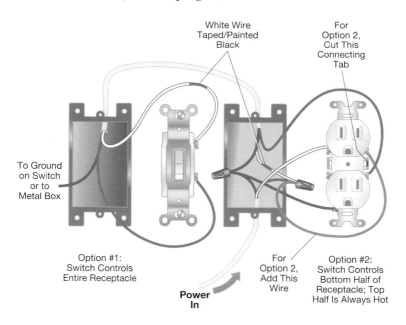

White Wire Taped/Painted Black

For Option 2, Cut This Connecting Tab

To Ground on Switch or to Metal Box

Option #1: Switch Controls Entire Receptacle

For Option 2, Add This Wire

Power In

Option #2: Switch Controls Bottom Half of Receptacle; Top Half Is Always Hot

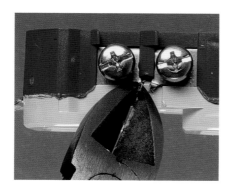

ONE HALF "HOT," ONE HALF SWITCHED. Take a close look at a household receptacle and you'll find a metal link between the screw terminals. If you cut this link (as shown in the photo at left), you can wire each plug-in separately.

To wire an end-of-run receptacle, connect the black wire to the brass screw terminal, the white to the silver terminal, and the ground wire to the ground lug. For a middle-of-run receptacle, see below.

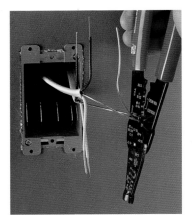 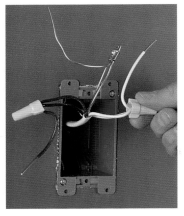

1 CONNECT THE GROUNDS. Pigtail the ground wires together with a compression sleeve or wire nut.

2 SPLICE THE HOT AND NEUTRAL WIRES. Use wire nuts to pigtail together pairs of neutral and hot wires: white to white, black to black.

3 CONNECT WIRES TO THE RECEPTACLE. Loop the ends of the pigtails with needle-nose pliers and secure them to the screw terminals. Alternatively, instead of pigtailing, you can attach pairs of hot and neutral wires to the pairs of screw terminals.

Mounting Switches/Receptacles

Once you've made your connections to a switch or receptacle, the last thing to do is attach it to the box and add a cover plate.

SECURE THE SWITCH OR RECEPTACLE. Standard switches and receptacles have two built-in mounting screws that are driven into threaded holes in a box. Before you can secure the switch or receptacle, you'll need to press it (and its wiring) carefully into the box. Press the wires in gently to keep from pulling a wire out of a wire nut and breaking a connection.

ADD THE COVER PLATE. Once you've secured the switch or receptacle, add the cover plate. Drive in the screw just enough to hold the plate in place; over-tightening will only cause the plate to crack.

P R O   T I P

Grades of Cover Plates

 Not all cover plates are the same. A commercial or "pro" version (bottom plate in photo) tends to be thicker and better-supported around the mounting hole. These stouter plates will crack less and stand up better over time. The cost difference between a standard plate and a "pro" plate is pennies—a worthwhile investment.

ELECTRICAL KNOW-HOW

Installing a GFCI Receptacle

GFCI receptacles detect small variations in current flow between the two legs of a circuit. When an imbalance occurs, the GFCI will shut off the power to the receptacle almost instantaneously. If you're updating wiring or installing new circuits, GFCI receptacles are required by most codes in all bathrooms, kitchens, garages, crawl spaces, unfinished basements, and outdoor receptacles.

1 REMOVE OLD RECEP-TACLE. First, turn off and tag power at the service panel. Remove the cover plate and unscrew the receptacle mounting screws. Gently pull out the old receptacle, loosen each of the screw terminals, and unhook the wires.

2 INSTALL THE GFCI. If this is a single-protection recep-tacle, attach the existing wires to the LINE screw terminals. For multiple-location protection (see page 89), con-

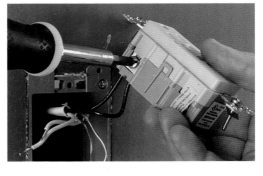

nect the incoming wires to the LINE screw terminals, and the line to be protected to the LOAD screw terminals.

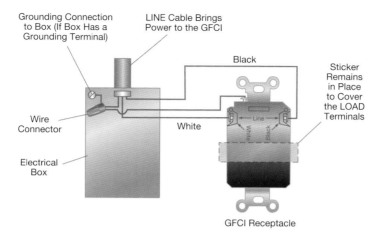

Grounding Connection to Box (If Box Has a Grounding Terminal)

LINE Cable Brings Power to the GFCI

Black

Sticker Remains in Place to Cover the LOAD Terminals

Wire Connector

White

Electrical Box

GFCI Receptacle

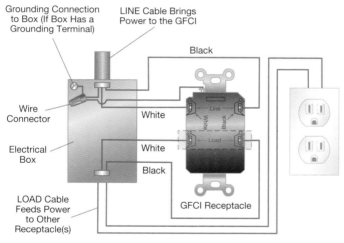

Grounding Connection to Box (If Box Has a Grounding Terminal)

LINE Cable Brings Power to the GFCI

Black

Wire Connector

White

Electrical Box

White

Black

LOAD Cable Feeds Power to Other Receptacle(s)

GFCI Receptacle

GFCI receptacles can be wired to protect just themselves or to protect all wiring, switches, and fixtures forward of the GFCI to the end of the circuit. Multiple-location protection is susceptible to erroneous tripping when normal fluctuations occur. If you must wire a GFCI to protect multiple locations, follow the directions carefully. Miswiring can leave both the outlet and the line you intend to protect without any ground-fault protection.

ELECTRICAL KNOW-HOW

Working with Flexible Metal Conduit

Armor-clad cable is a flexible metal conduit that can carry two, three, or four conductors. Since armor-clad cable is restricted in many areas, check with your local building inspector before installing it in your house. When you cut armor-clad cable, you'll end up with a jagged end that can damage the conductors inside. Cable connectors save the day by providing a smooth transition for the conductors—there are two types: screw-in and clamp-on.

SCREW-IN CONNECTORS. The best way to protect conductors from the jagged end of armor-clad cable is to screw in a connector at the end of the cable.

CLAMP-ON CONNECTORS. With a clamp-on connector, the armor-clad cable is inserted into the clamp and secured with a pair of screws. The one shown here is designed to mount onto a metal electrical box.

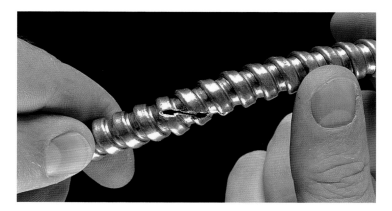

CUTTING FLEXIBLE CONDUIT. Start by clamping the cable securely to a sawhorse or workbench and mark the cut. Then, with a hacksaw held at a right angle to the spirals in the cable, cut into the sheathing at the mark. Stop as soon as you've passed through the sheathing. Now twist the armor until it snaps. Then cut through the spiral with electrician's pliers.

CONNECTING TO BOXES. Flexible metal conduit is readily attached to a metal box using clamp-on connectors. Two different styles allow the cable either to enter straight into the box, or to enter at a right angle (as shown here).

Working with Rigid Metal Conduit

Rigid metal conduit protects wiring that's attached to the exterior of a wall. It's readily cut with a hacksaw or a tubing cutter. It can be easily bent as needed with a conduit bender to go around corners (page 95). Although it can be challenging to produce the desired bend, a simple job without a lot of bends is something almost any homeowner can handle. If you're planning on bending a lot of conduit, it's a good idea to buy a couple of extra lengths and practice bending it before tackling your project. The first step to installing rigid metal conduit is to locate and mount any electrical boxes. Then you'll measure, cut, and bend the conduit to run from box to box.

CUTTING CONDUIT. With a tape measure, measure from box to box or from a box to a connector. Then subtract the length of any connectors you'll be using. Transfer this measurement to the conduit and make a mark. Then cut it to length with a tubing cutter or hacksaw.

SMOOTH THE CUT ENDS. Next, remove any sharp edges on the cut ends that could cut into sheathing or insulation. Use a reamer (as shown here) or file to smooth the inside edges.

JOINING WITH CONNECTORS. It's easy to join together lengths of conduit. Just slip a through connector over the ends and tighten the lock-down screws.

JOINING TO BOXES. When conduit enters a box, you'll usually want to add an offset (as shown here). This is a connector that has a slight jog in it and serves as a transition between the box and the wall covering; it lets the conduit lie flat against the wall.

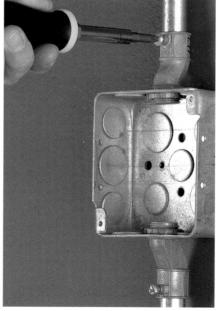

Bending conduit with precision requires practice—make sure to buy extra lengths for any project you're planning.

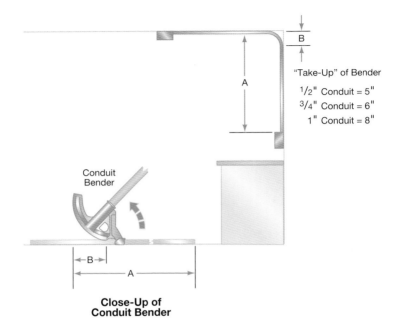

"Take-Up" of Bender

$1/2$" Conduit = 5"
$3/4$" Conduit = 6"
1" Conduit = 8"

Conduit Bender

Close-Up of Conduit Bender

LAYING OUT A BEND. The first step to bending conduit around a corner is to take some measurements. With a tape measure, measure out from the wall or ceiling to a box (drawing above). Then subtract the length of any offsets or connectors you'll be using. You'll also need to subtract the "take-up" of the bender from this length (typically 5" for $1/2$" conduit, 6" for $3/4$" conduit, and 8" for 1" conduit). Take-up is how much conduit the bender needs to create a radius. It's generally safer to cut the conduit long, make the bend, and then trim it to fit.

USING A CONDUIT BENDER.
Here's the tricky part—positioning the bender on the conduit. Start by making a mark on the conduit equal to the distance "A" shown in the drawing on page 94. Then subtract the "take-up" ("B") from this and make a mark. This is the mark you'll want to line up with the alignment mark on the conduit bender. Place one foot on the "pedal" of the bender and with firm, gentle pressure, slowly pull the handle toward you. Gentle pressure is essential here, as it's

very easy to crimp the conduit. Most benders have a built-in bubble level to let you know when you've reached 90 degrees.

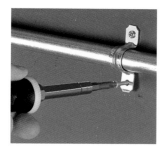

SECURE WITH STRAPS.
Because of its weight, conduit must be securely fastened to wall studs and framing members to prevent it from pulling on boxes and fixtures. Use cable straps to secure the conduit every few feet and especially near any curves.

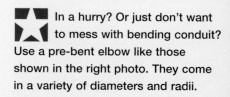

P R O   T I P

Pre-Bent Elbows

In a hurry? Or just don't want to mess with bending conduit? Use a pre-bent elbow like those shown in the right photo. They come in a variety of diameters and radii.

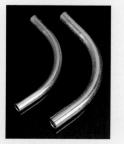

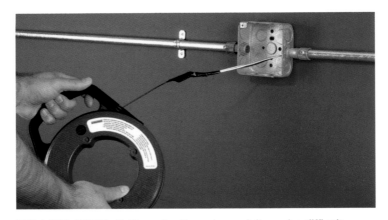

PULLING WIRE. Pulling wire through conduit can be difficult—especially if there are a lot of bends, the run is long, or you're running the maximum number of allowable wires through the conduit. For short runs where the wire doesn't have many turns, it's possible to push the wire to its destination. If you try this, tape the wire together at the end and about every 6" for the first foot. This creates a more solid package that's easier to push. Taping the end also prevents the individual wires from catching on edges of connector and boxes. For longer or complex runs, have a helper push the cable or wire and use a fish tape to pull the wire to its destination.

PRO TIP

Cable Lube

For complex runs, pros turn to cable lube to help the cable slide through the conduit. To use cable lube, apply a generous amount to the wire as it enters the electrical box. Continue applying lubricant until you can feel the wire work past the problem area. At that point you can stop lubricating, as what's already in the conduit will get the job done.

Working with Plastic Conduit

Although plastic conduit doesn't protect wires as well as metal conduit, it's a whole lot easier to work with. It can be easily cut with a hacksaw, handsaw, or power saw, and the conduit and fittings cement together to create strong, watertight joints.

REAM THE ENDS. Once you've cut a piece of plastic conduit to length, take the time to ream the inside edges smooth with a utility knife or reamer. A smooth inside edge can't abrade cable sheathing.

Cement the joints

There are a couple of steps to creating a strong joint with plastic conduit: prime and cement, and insert and twist.

1 APPLY PRIMER AND CEMENT. Although not absolutely necessary, you'll get a better bond if you first apply PVC primer to the conduit and fitting before swabbing on a generous coat of cement.

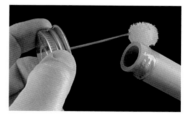

2 INSERT AND TWIST. Insert the plastic conduit into the fitting until it hits the internal stop. Then give the pipe or fitting a quarter-turn to help evenly distribute the cement. Allow the cement to set the recommended time before adding other fittings.

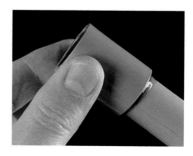

ELECTRICAL KNOW-HOW

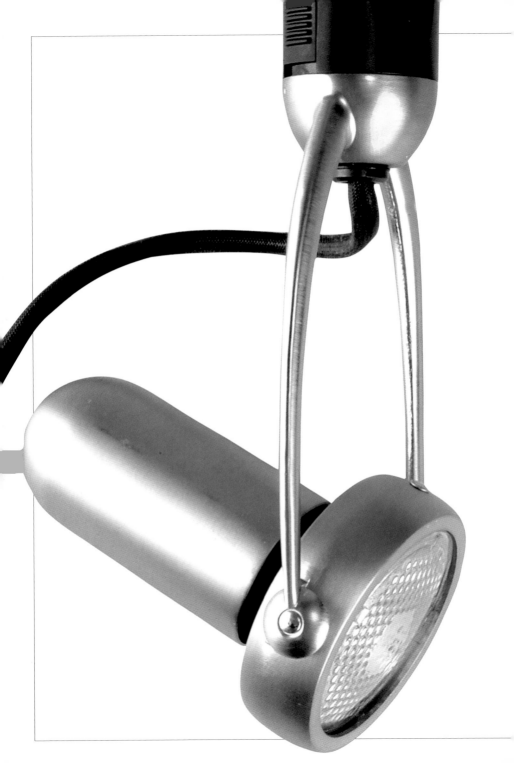

5

Lighting Projects

LIKE FEW OTHER ELECTRICAL PROJECTS, lighting turns on big impact for relatively small effort and cost. To brighten, create a mood, or accent a feature in almost any room, try your hand at any of the projects here: installing incandescent and fluorescent fixtures, track lighting, a decorative wall sconce, recessed lighting, under-cabinet lighting, low-voltage exterior lighting, and dimmer switches, plus lamp repair.

A New Incandescent Fixture

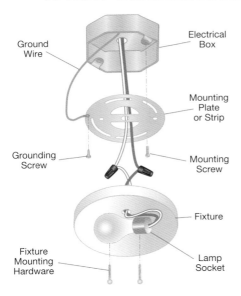

Ground Wire

Electrical Box

Mounting Plate or Strip

Grounding Screw

Mounting Screw

Fixture

Fixture Mounting Hardware

Lamp Socket

The simplest lighting project is to replace an existing overhead fixture with a new one. Electrical connections involve two wires and a ground (drawing at left). There are, though, a few things to keep in mind. First, make sure the new lighting fixture will fit and that it doesn't hang too low. Second, the ceiling-mounted electrical box must be able to handle the weight of the new fixture. Lightweight fixtures can be supported by just the box; heavy fixtures need the box to be attached to framing members.

QUICK FIX

Ceiling Medallions

A common problem when replacing an overhead fixture is that the base plate of the new fixture is smaller than the old one. This can leave an unsightly portion of the ceiling exposed. You could patch and paint this area, but a more elegant solution is to install a medallion. Not

only does this cover up the problem area, but it also adds a distinctive touch to both the ceiling and the new light fixture.

Severing Paint Bonds

If the old fixture doesn't come off easily, it's probably "glued" in place with old paint. If you pull off the fixture without severing the paint bond, you'll likely damage the ceiling. So run the blade of a utility knife or putty knife around the edges of the old fixture base to free it from old caulk or paint.

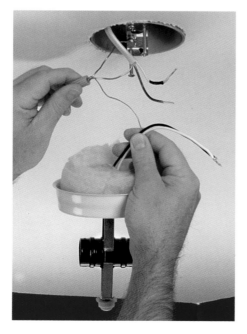

1 REMOVE THE OLD FIXTURE. Start by turning off the power to the fixture and tagging the panel. Then remove the globe or diffuser and the lightbulb(s). Next, unscrew the retaining nut that holds the fixture plate to the electrical box. Pull the fixture away from the box, unscrew the wire nuts, separate the wires, and set the fixture aside.

LIGHTING PROJECTS

2 INSTALL NEW MOUNTING STRAP.
Electrical code requires that all fixtures be mounted to a flat metal bar called a mounting strap or plate that is secured to the box. Most new fixtures include a mounting strap. Fasten the strap to the box with the screws provided.

3 WIRE NEW FIXTURE.
Before you install the new fixture, inspect the existing wires. If the insulation is cracked or the ends are nicked or tarnished, cut off the ends and strip off insulation with a wire stripper. Then attach the new fixture wires to the existing wires with the wire nuts supplied.

GROUNDING A MOUNTING STRAP

✚ For safety, grounding straps must be connected to the circuit's ground wires. You'll find a ground lug on the strap just for this. To minimize clutter inside the box, it's best to pigtail (page 65) the circuit ground wire to the fixture's ground and connect the pigtail to the mounting strap's ground lug.

4 **MOUNT THE FIXTURE.** Attach the fixture to the mounting plate with the hardware provided. If you'll be installing a medallion (see page 100), do so before attaching the fixture.

5 **ADD LAMPS AND DIFFUSER.** Screw in the appropriate bulbs and attach the diffuser. The diffuser is typically held in place with a decorative cap or retaining nut. Tighten this friction-tight and no more—over-tightening can easily crack the diffuser.

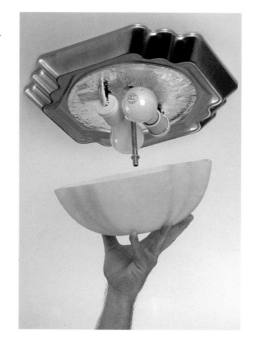

Installing Track Lighting

Track lighting provides customizable accent lighting in your home; individual lamps snap into a track anywhere along its length to spotlight different areas of the room. You can replace an existing fixture with track lighting or have a new electrical box installed to add lighting to a new area in your home. The simplest way to buy track lighting is to purchase a kit. A kit usually includes: a mounting plate with wiring hub that attaches to the electrical box, a track that attaches to the mounting plate and ceiling, a connector housing cover, and separate lighting fixtures (drawing below).

1 WIRE THE MOUNTING PLATE. To install track lighting, start by turning off power to the existing fixture. Remove the old fixture and connect the existing wiring to the wiring hub on the new mounting plate, using the wire nuts provided.

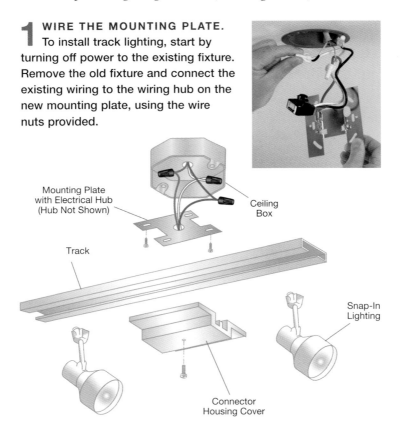

Mounting Plate with Electrical Hub (Hub Not Shown)

Ceiling Box

Track

Snap-In Lighting

Connector Housing Cover

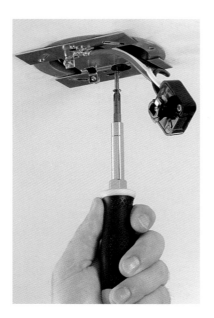

2 ATTACH THE MOUNTING PLATE.

Carefully tuck all the wires up into the electrical box and screw the mounting plate to the box. Note: Some mounting plates (like the one shown here) have a pair of setscrews on the connector housing to grip the track. This is important because how you orient the mounting plate on the box will also orient the track on the ceiling.

3 INSTALL THE TRACK.

Temporarily secure the track to the mounting plate and mark the track's mounting hole locations on the ceiling. Remove the track and drill holes for the toggle bolts or plastic anchors (often supplied with the kit) that will secure the track to the ceiling. Install the anchors, hold the track in position, and screw it to the ceiling.

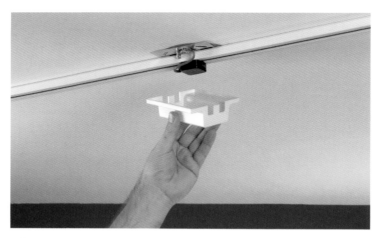

4 ADD THE MOUNTING PLATE COVER. Once the track is secured, place the cover over the mounting plate and track and fasten it to the mounting plate with the screws provided.

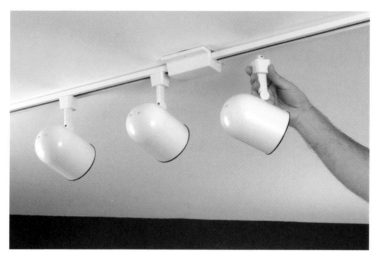

5 ADD THE FIXTURES. Unpack the individual light fixtures and install them in the track at the desired locations. In most cases, a connector on the end of each lamp fits into the track; then you rotate it to snap it in place and make electrical contact with the track. Finally, add bulbs, restore power, and test. Adjust the fixtures to get the desired lighting effect.

A New Fluorescent Fixture

Most overhead fluorescent fixtures go up as easily as incandescent fixtures (pages 100–103). The big difference: The base on a fluorescent fixture tends to be heavier than an incandescent base. That's because it holds the ballast that generates the higher voltage necessary for fluorescent tubes to light.

1 WIRE THE FIXTURE. Remove the old fixture, attach the mounting strap, and connect the new fixture's wires to the existing wires with the wire nuts provided.

2 ATTACH THE FIXTURE. Push the wiring gently up into the box and secure the base to the mounting strap with the screws supplied.

3 ADD THE LAMP AND DIFFUSER. Install the fluorescent bulb or bulbs and attach the diffuser with the hardware provided.

Adding a Wall Sconce

Adding a wall sconce can be straightforward or challenging, depending on where you mount the control switch and fixture. The simplest way is to tap into power at a nearby receptacle and position both the switch and fixture directly above the receptacle. By locating everything between the same pair of wall studs, you don't have to cut access holes and drill through any plates, as you would if you sited the switch or fixture away from the receptacle. This is still do-able; see page 110. The sconce itself is easy to install (drawing below).

1 CUT HOLES FOR SWITCH BOXES. Once you've identified the receptacle you're going to extend, locate a box for the control switch and one for the fixture. See page 72 for guidelines on locating switches; where you locate the fixture box is your call. See pages 74–75 for more on installing boxes.

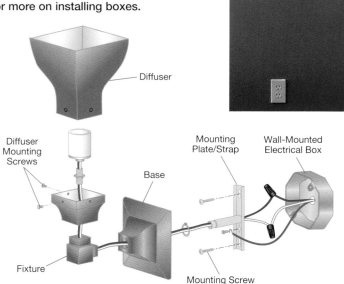

Diffuser

Diffuser Mounting Screws

Base

Fixture

Mounting Plate/Strap

Wall-Mounted Electrical Box

Mounting Screw

2 REMOVE THE RECEPTACLE AND BOX. Turn off the power and tag the main panel. Remove the cover plate of the receptacle you'll be extending and the receptacle mounting screws. Gently pull the receptacle, loosen the screws, disconnect the wires, and set the receptacle aside. Loosen the cable clamp and pull the box out of the wall if possible to make it easier to fish the new cable. Alternatively, leave it in place and fish the cable through a box opening.

3 FISH CABLE FROM RECEPTACLE TO SWITCH BOX. Attach a 2-wire cable to a fish tape and pull the new cable from the receptacle to the hole for the switch box. Make sure to leave yourself plenty of excess cable.

4 FISH CABLE FROM SWITCH TO THE FIXTURE. Attach a 3-wire cable to a fish tape and pull it from the switch box up to the hole you cut for the fixture box.

SITING THE SWITCH OR SCONCE AWAY FROM EXISTING RECEPTACLE. If you want to locate your wall sconce away from the receptacle, you'll need to cut holes in the walls to access the top or bottom plate so you can drill holes in them for fishing the cable (see page 70 for more on this). Then you can fish the cable up into the attic or down into the basement or crawl space to get it to the desired location.

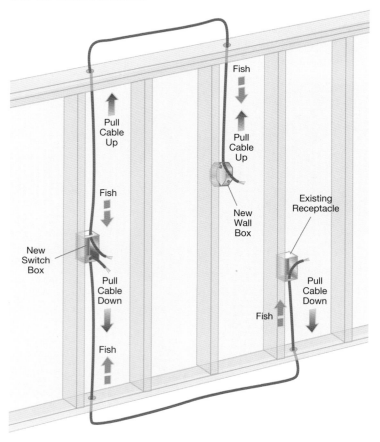

5 INSTALL THE BOXES.
Insert the cable (or cables) into a box and secure it with the cable clamp (if applicable). Then insert it into the hole in the wall and secure with the built-in clamps.

6 WIRE THE SWITCH.
Remove the cable sheathing, strip the wires, and prepare them for screw terminals. Attach the wires to the switch (as described on pages 78–83). Press the switch gently into its box and secure both ends with mounting screws. Then attach a cover plate.

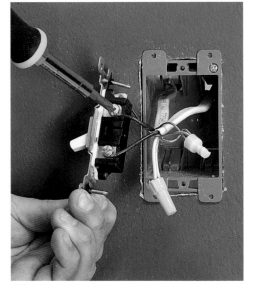

7 **ATTACH THE FIX-TURE MOUNTING PLATE.** Most new fixtures include a mounting strap (or you can buy a "universal" mounting strap at your hardware store). Fasten the strap to the box with the screws provided.

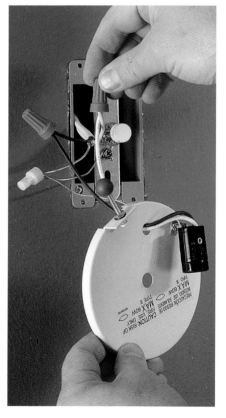

8 **CONNECT THE FIXTURE.** Connect the fixture's wires to the cable wires coming up from the control switch, as described on pages 78–83.

9 **MOUNT THE FIXTURE.** Push the wiring into the electrical box and secure the fixture to the mounting plate, using the screws or nuts supplied.

10 **ADD THE DIFFUSER.** Finally, screw in the appropriate bulb or bulbs. Make sure the bulbs you are using have a wattage rating less than or equal to the maximum allowable rating for the fixture. Then attach the diffuser; it's usually held in place with a decorative cap or retaining nut. Tighten this friction-tight and no more.

LIGHTING PROJECTS

Recessed Lighting

Recessed lights let you put light exactly where you need it. They're designed for mounting in one of three ways: in a suspended ceiling, in new construction, or in remodel work. Recessed lights are either single units (see the drawing below) or two-piece units con-

sisting of a mounting frame and a light.

It's easy to differentiate between a new-construction light and a remodel light. New-construction lights typically sport a pair of adjustable slides that attach to ceiling joists (left light in photo). Remodel lights are streamlined to fit into the new holes cut into the ceiling (right light in photo) and are held in place with clips. (For more on mounting new-construction lights, see page 119.) Finally, if your ceiling

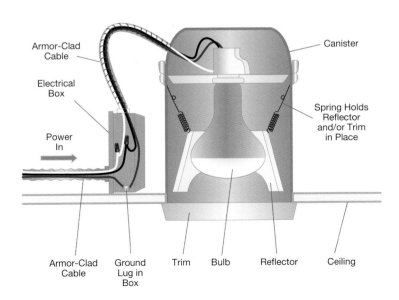

Armor-Clad Cable

Electrical Box

Power In

Canister

Spring Holds Reflector and/or Trim in Place

Armor-Clad Cable Ground Lug in Box Trim Bulb Reflector Ceiling is insulated, as most are, be sure to buy lights that are rated for contact with insulation. Otherwise, you'll need to clear out insulation (see page 117), and hot and cool air will escape through this un-insulated portion.

1 LOCATE THE CEILING JOISTS.
The first step in installing a recessed light is to identify where you want the light. Then locate the ceiling joists with a stud finder.

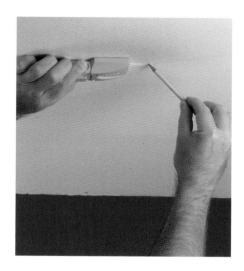

2 MARK HOLE IN CEILING. Whenever possible, locate the light between joists to provide plenty of clearance during installation. Mark the hole for the light on the ceiling using either the template provided or a compass set to the desired radius.

LIGHTING PROJECTS

3 CUT THE HOLE IN THE CEILING. Use a drywall saw or a reciprocating saw to cut the opening for the light in the ceiling. Clear out any insulation to make room for the fixture. If your light is a two-piece model, separate the parts as directed and drop the can through the frame. Then push the frame through the hole in the ceiling and attach it to the ceiling with the remodel clips provided (see page 118).

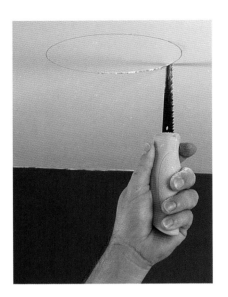

P R O   T I P

Large Hole Saws

For a recessed remodel light to fit properly in the ceiling hole, the hole must be cut accurately. Pros often carry one or more large hole saws (photo below) sized for various lights. These are particularly useful when cutting into materials other than drywall, such as a wood soffit above a sink. The only drawback to these is cost: The 6" hole saw at left will set you back around $45.

✚ It's generally best to buy IC-rated (insulation contact) lighting. These lights are designed to work safely in direct contact with ceiling insulation. With non-IC-rated lights, you need to push insulation away from the light (typically 3" to 6"); that effectively creates a hole in your ceiling for warm or cool air to flow out.

4 **WIRE THE FIXTURE.** The next step is to run power to the light; the simplest way is to route the power cable of the old overhead light to the new location. This way, the existing light switch can control the lights. If this isn't possible, run new lines (see pages 182–187) or have them installed by an electrician. When you have power routed to the light, follow the manufacturer's directions to wire the fixture.

5 **PUSH LIGHT UP INTO CEILING.** Push the light up through the hole and into the ceiling. For two-piece units, insert the light fixture through the frame you mounted earlier.

LIGHTING PROJECTS

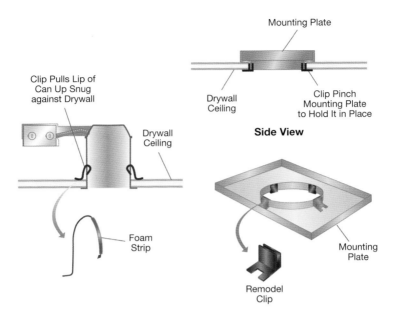

Mounting Plate

Clip Pulls Lip of
Can Up Snug
against Drywall

Drywall
Ceiling

Clip Pinch
Mounting Plate
to Hold It in Place

Drywall
Ceiling

Side View

Foam
Strip

Mounting
Plate

Remodel
Clip

6 **SECURE THE LIGHT TO THE CEILING.** For one-piece
light units (like the one shown here), slide the built-in spring
clips up into the can with a pair of needle-nose pliers. You want
the clips to pivot out over the ceiling to pull the lip of the fixture

firmly into the ceiling
(drawing above). With
two-piece units, the light
commonly attaches to the
mounting frame via a set
of screws. As mentioned
earlier, the frame is secured
to the ceiling with small
remodel clips.

7 ADD THE TRIM.
All that's left is to add the decorative trim to the fixture. There are many different ways trim is held in place. On some models, the trim is simply pushed up into the fixture and spring clips hold it in place. Other lights use long springs that must be hooked onto tabs

up inside the fixture to secure the trim. Some recessed lights feature a separate bulb holder which may need to be threaded into a socket up inside the light before installing the trim. Otherwise, just screw the bulb into the lamp, restore power, and test the light.

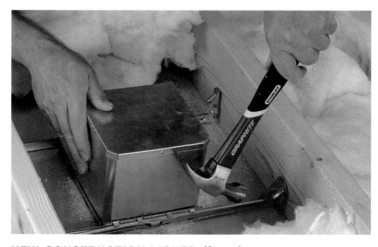

NEW-CONSTRUCTION LIGHTS. If you have easy access to your ceiling from above, you can install new-construction lights. These are much more secure than remodel lights because they're secured to the ceiling joists. Just adjust the slides so they contact the joists and secure them with screws or nails (as shown here).

Under-Cabinet Lighting

Under-cabinet lighting can be as simple as installing a single strip light underneath cabinets, or as complex as adding a series of puck lights, either as task lighting or as an accent. Although you can mount an under-cabinet light anywhere underneath the cabinet, most manufacturers recommend locating the strip or pucks as close to the front of the cabinet as possible for the best coverage.

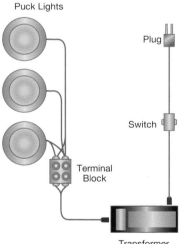

Strips are easy to install, but some areas just don't need an entire strip of lights. Here's where small, individual "puck"-shaped halogen lights are ideal. Puck lights are available in packs of two or more; you mount them exactly where you need the light and then wire them together. Wiring is simple: The wiring just snaps into each light (drawing above). Most under-cabinet fixtures are designed to plug into a wall receptacle. Halogen fixtures typically require adding a low-voltage transformer that plugs into a standard receptacle.

1 INSTALL THE BASE. Each puck light usually consists of two or more parts: a base and/or fixture that's secured to the underside of the cabinet, and a separate lens. When you've determined the best position for the light, locate and mark the holes for the mounting hardware. Using the recommended-sized drill bit, drill pilot holes for the screws (supplied with most lights) and drive in the screws through the base or fixture into the cabinet bottom.

Dealing with Stripped Screws

If you happen to strip a screw while installing a base or fixture, try this simple fix. Glue one or more wood toothpicks into the stripped hole. Then drive in the screw—the toothpicks will provide a new grip for the screw threads.

Stripped/Enlarged Screw Hole

Glue/Insert Toothpicks in Hole

Toothpicks Provide "Grip" for Screw Threads

LIGHTING PROJECTS

2 ADD THE LENS. Once you've installed all the puck bases or fixtures, go back and snap the lens covers in place.

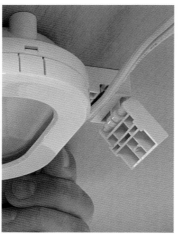

3 CONNECT EACH PUCK TO POWER. Most puck lights have some form of quick-connect feature that lets you quickly add the wiring. Some have male and female clips. Others (like the ones shown here) use a press-together system. With this system, you insert the power cord in one half of the connector as shown. When you flip the hinged cover over and snap it in place, it forces sharp prongs inside the connector to penetrate the cable and make a solid connection.

4 ROUTE THE POWER CORD. Most puck kits include nail-in cable clamps so that you can conceal the power cord by routing it up under the lip of the cabinet as shown.

5 ADD THE SWITCH AND PLUG IN. All that's left is to install the power switch following the manufacturer's directions, plug in the power cord, and test.

Self-Adhesive Cable Clamps

The tiny nail-in cable clamps that most kits contain often don't hold the power cable very securely. You can pick up beefier self-adhesive cable clamps (like the ones shown here) at most hardware stores and home centers. They install without any fuss and will hold the cable secure.

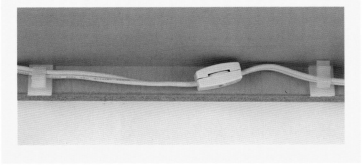

LIGHTING PROJECTS

3 **CONNECT LAMPS TO THE POWER CABLE.** After you've positioned the lights, run the power cable. Start at the light farthest away from the outdoor receptacle, and run the cable back toward the receptacle. Almost all low-voltage lighting systems use a two-piece snap-together connector; each half fits on one side of the power cable. When the two halves of the connector are squeezed together, sharp prongs inside the connector halves pierce the insulation of the power cable to make a solid electrical connection.

4 **BURY THE CABLE.** With all the connections made, work your way from light to light, digging a shallow trench, inserting the cable, and covering it up. Most manufacturers provide a recommended maximum depth that you can bury the cable (drawing at right).

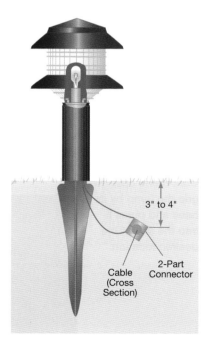

3" to 4"

Cable (Cross Section)

2-Part Connector

5 CONNECT THE POWER CABLE.

Follow the manufacturer's directions to attach the cable to the transformer. These may be push- or snap-in terminals, or screw terminals (as shown here). Then attach the transformer to the wall nearest the receptacle (these usually hang on screws driven into the wall), and plug the transformer's power cord into the receptacle. Note: If the receptacle is exposed to the elements, you'll need to install a weatherproof cover—these are available wherever electrical supplies are sold.

6 SET THE TIMER.

Finally, follow the manufacturer's directions on setting the timer. This usually entails placing a set of plastic stops along the edge of a rotating timer at the desired on and off intervals.

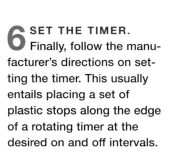

LIGHTING PROJECTS

Lamp Repair

You flip on a lamp and nothing happens. You replace the bulb—same thing. What now? Don't toss it—repair it. Lamp repair is easy because lamps are simple devices. Most lamps consist of a socket, a switch, and a cord (drawing below). Major problem areas are the cord/plug and the only electro-mechanical part of the lamp: the switch and socket (which are subjected to constant use). See pages 202–203 for how to troubleshoot lamp problems.

LEVER-STYLE PLUGS. To replace a plug, first identify the cord. Flat cords (also called zip cords) have two wires, encased in insulation, that are easily "zipped" apart. This type of cord will accept a lever-style plug (shown below) or a standard plug (see page 129). Round cords, with their thicker conductors, can handle more current and accept heavy-duty plugs (see page 130). Separate the two conductors about 1¼". For round cords, remove 1¼" of sheathing. Then strip off insulation and open the plug. Wrap one conductor around each screw and tighten. Close the casing and secure it.

Socket Shell

Harp

Insulating Sleeve

Socket

Socket Cap

Harp Socket

Lamp Base

Power Cord and Plug

Standard plugs

Standard plugs usually have two parts: an inner plug with screw terminals, and the casing it fits inside.

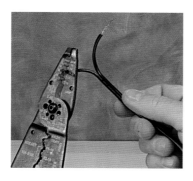

1 **PREPARE THE CORD.** When working with flat or "zip" cord, separate the conductors and remove about ¾" of insulation from each end. If you're reusing a round cord, check the condition of the wires. If they're tarnished or broken, cut the ends off and restrip (you may need to remove some of the outer insulation to expose sufficient lengths of the inner conductors). If you're using a two-part plug, slip the casing over the cord now.

QUICK FIX

Underwriter's Knot

For plugs that don't have built-in strain relief—and for added pull-out protection for even for those plugs that do—tie the conductors together with a special "underwriter's knot," as shown. After you've tied the knot, pull the ends of the con-

ductors to tighten the knot. Check to make sure the knot will do its job as a strain relief by pulling the knot down and into the plug housing. If you can still pull it through, you'll need to purchase a small clamp to fit around the section where the cord passes out of the housing. Tightening the clamp will compress the sleeve and grip the cord.

LIGHTING PROJECTS

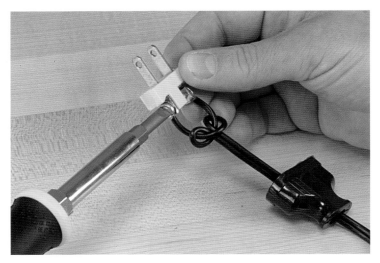

2 **CONNECT THE WIRES.** Wrap each conductor around the appropriate screw terminal. (If you're working with round cord: The black wire wraps around the brass screw, the white wire goes around the silver screw, and the green goes around the grounding screw.) Use a screwdriver to tighten the screws. Don't be tempted to over-tighten these—all you'll accomplish is squishing the twisted strands.

3 **ASSEMBLE THE PLUG.** Slide the outer plug casing up onto the inner plug section and secure it with the screws provided. If your plug has a built-in strain relief (like the plug shown here), tighten it to pinch the cord. If you used an underwriter's knot, give the cord a tug to make sure it's providing sufficient strain relief.

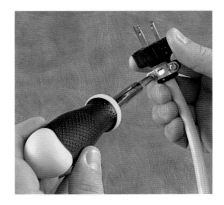

Commercial-Grade Plugs

■▼■
▶◣◤ Although not as streamlined or attractive as a standard plug, pros often replace standard plugs on lamps and other hardworking devices that are subjected to a lot of wear and tear with heavy-duty commercial-grade versions. These stout plugs feature bulked-up parts made of high-impact plastic and extra-strong strain reliefs.

Replacing a switch/socket assembly

The toughest part of replacing a switch/socket assembly is finding an exact replacement part. If you can't find what you need at your hardware store or home center, try a lighting or electrical supply house.

1 **REMOVE THE COVER.** To replace a lamp's switch/socket assembly, start by removing the socket cover. This may twist off (as shown here) or need to be pried off (as is the case with most metal sockets).

LIGHTING PROJECTS

2 RELEASE THE WIRING. There's often not enough slack in the power cord for you to pull the socket out at this time. You'll typically need to remove a cover plate (as shown here) or loosen the lamp's strain relief in order to provide

this much-needed slack. When you've got sufficient slack in the power cord, gently ease the socket out of its case far enough to expose its screw terminals.

3 REPLACE THE SOCKET. To replace the socket, first loosen the terminal screws and pull the wires off; set the old socket aside. Wrap the existing wires around the terminals of the new socket and tighten them with a screwdriver. Reverse the disassembly process to re-assemble the lamp.

Installing a Dimmer Switch

Want to change the mood in a room without replacing a light fixture? Just install a dimmer switch to vary a light's brightness. The only tricky part is getting the larger-bodied switch to fit inside the existing box.

1 REMOVE THE OLD SWITCH. Turn off the power and tag the main panel. Remove the cover plate and mounting screws. Gently pull out the switch and disconnect each wire with a screwdriver.

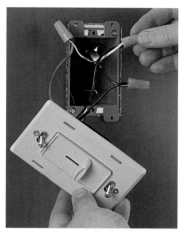

2 WIRE THE DIMMER SWITCH. Dimmer switches often use wire leads for connections instead of screws. Use wire nuts to connect the switch wires to the circuit wires. These wires are interchangeable, so you can connect them to either wire lead.

3 MOUNT THE NEW SWITCH. Gently push the dimmer switch into the box. Install the mounting screws and cover plate, restore the power, and test.

LIGHTING PROJECTS

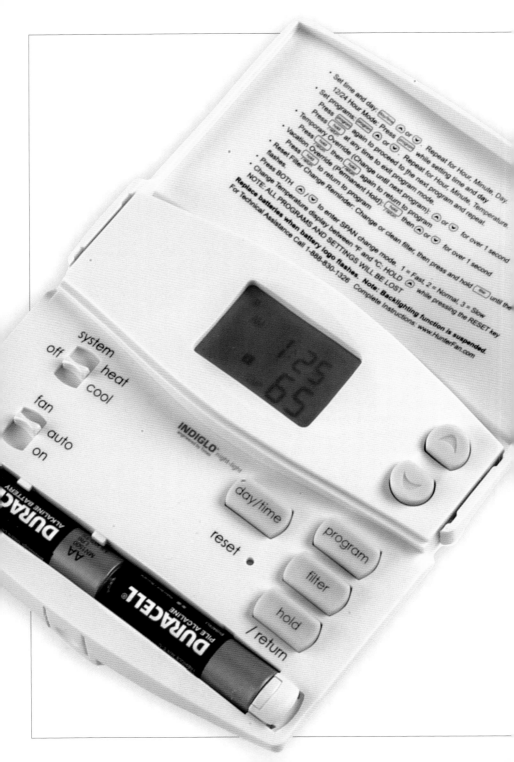

6

Heating and Cooling Projects

TECHNOLOGY HELPS US warm our homes in winter and cool them in summer—and it's also technology that helps keep heating and cooling costs down. In this chapter, we'll use technology to advantage in three energy-smart projects: installing a ceiling fan, adding a bathroom fan, and installing a programmable thermostat.

Installing a Ceiling Fan

A ceiling fan can cool in the summer and heat in the winter. That's right—heat. While it has no heating element, a ceiling fan set on low in the downdraft mode can actually help drive warm air from near the ceiling down into the living space to create a more uniformly heated room. All ceiling fans have similar parts and are usually wired to an existing switch. If you want a ceiling fan without having to install a new switch, look for a model with a remote control or a pull-chain on/off switch.

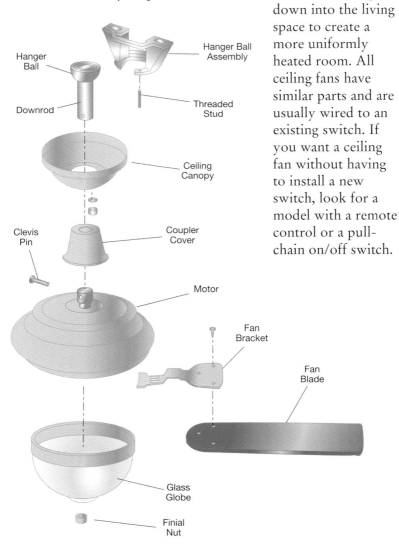

Hanger Ball

Hanger Ball Assembly

Downrod

Threaded Stud

Ceiling Canopy

Clevis Pin

Coupler Cover

Motor

Fan Bracket

Fan Blade

Glass Globe

Finial Nut

Common parts include a mounting plate or hanger ball assembly, an optional down-rod, a canopy, the fan motor, fan brackets, blades, and option lighting (drawing on page 136).

Fitting a Fan to a Room

BLADE SIZE	ROOM SIZE	SQUARE FOOTAGE
36"	10 × 10	100 sq. ft.
42"	12 × 12	144 sq. ft.
44" or 48"	15 × 15	225 sq. ft.
52" or 54"	20 × 20	400 sq. ft.
56"	22 × 22	485 sq. ft.
60"	25 × 25	625 sq. ft.

Fan sizes

Ceiling fans are rated to match the size of the room. Just measure your room and pick the blade size that best matches your space; see the chart above.

Mounting options

There are three ways to mount most ceiling fans: flush, standard, and angled. The type you choose will depend on the height and slope of your ceiling. The general rule of thumb is that you need at least 7 feet of clearance between the fan blades and the floor.

Screw Directly
to Bottom of Joist

Screw to
Side of Joist

CEILING BOXES. Because ceiling fans are heavy, they must be installed in electrical boxes especially designed to handle this weight (see the drawing at right), or attach to heavy-duty boxes affixed directly to your ceiling joist (see page 138). The style you choose will depend on the access you have to the box.

Low-Profile
Plastic Box Fits
over Joist and
Is Screwed to
Bottom

Ceiling brackets

When you don't have access to the ceiling from above, you'll need to work from below. There's a nifty fixture available just for situations like this: It consists of a threaded bar that accepts an electrical box. (Note: A similar style of bracket is available for new-construction work as well; see the drawing at right.)

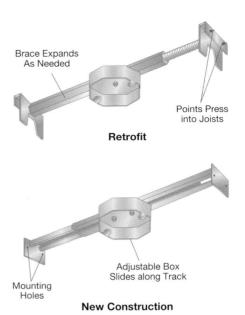

Brace Expands As Needed

Points Press into Joists

Retrofit

Mounting Holes

Adjustable Box Slides along Track

New Construction

1 **INSERT THE BAR.** To install a ceiling bracket, start by removing the box. Set it aside, then insert the bar through the hole in the ceiling.

2 **TIGHTEN TO LOCK IN PLACE.** Position the bar so that it's perpendicular to the ceiling joists. Rotate the bar so that it lengthens and drives the barbed end brackets into the ceiling joists. Then reattach the box.

Although fan installation is similar from brand to brand, follow the manufacturer's directions for your unit.

1 INSTALL THE MOUNTING PLATE.
Start by turning off the power and removing the old fixture. Then thread the electrical wires coming out of the box through the opening in the new mounting plate. Using the hardware provided, secure the mounting plate to the electrical box and/or ceiling joist as directed.

2 ATTACH THE BLADE BRACKETS. Before you hang the fan, most manufacturers will have you install the blade brackets. These usually screw directly into the rotor on the under-side of the fan motor.

3 **HANG THE FAN.** Since ceiling fans are heavy, most fan manufacturers have added a hook on the mounting plate to suspend the fan from so that you can connect the wires. If your ceiling plate has one of these, hook the fan onto it as shown in the photo at right. If it doesn't, enlist the aid of a helper to hold the fan while you connect the wires.

4 **CONNECT THE WIRING.** The wiring for most ceiling fans is pretty straightforward. Connect black to black and white to white. Connect the ground wire to the ground wire of the fan or to the grounding lug on the ceiling plate. Most fans come with wire nuts for making these connections.

5 **ATTACH MOTOR TO MOUNTING PLATE.** With the wiring complete, stuff the wires up through the opening in the mounting plate and into the electrical box. Unhook the fan and position it on the plate so the holes in the fan align with those in the mounting plate. Secure it with the screws provided. Here, the weight of the fan can make this difficult. Consider getting a helper to hold and align the fan while you drive in the mounting screws. Most fans have a canopy that slips over the fan housing to conceal the inner workings and keep out dust. If your fan has a canopy, slip it into place.

6 **INSTALL THE BLADES.** Blade-mounting systems can be either screw-on or snap-in. Attach the blades with the hardware supplied.

7 ADD THE LIGHT FIXTURE (OPTIONAL). If your fan has a light fixture, connect the socket to the bottom of the switch housing, following the manufacturer's instructions. Then secure the light fixture to the bottom of the fan unit.

8 ADD THE DIFFUSERS. All that's left is to add the diffusers. Again, mounting systems vary from brand to brand. On many fans, you slip a diffuser over a light socket and then thread on a plastic nut. With a more user-friendly system (like the one shown here), you just insert the diffuser in the lamp bracket and twist to lock it in place. Finally, restore power and test the fan. If the fan wobbles, see page 143 for how to fix this.

Blade-Balancing Kits

Don't be surprised if you turn on your new fan and it wobbles like a car in need of a front-end alignment. Most new fans need to be balanced, just as you balance new tires before installing them on your car. Many manufacturers include blade-balancing kits along with their fans (photo at right). Kits include directions, an adjustable clip, and self-adhesive weights.

1 ATTACH CLIP AND TEST. Turn off the fan and attach the clip to the leading edge of one blade halfway between the blade tip and the bracket. Run the fan and observe the wobble. Stop the fan and move the clip to the next blade; turn it on and observe the wobble. Repeat for the remaining blades. Now move the clip back to the blade with the least wobble, but this time attach the clip near the blade bracket. Turn on and observe. Stop the fan and move the clip out toward the blade tip in small increments until you find the position where the fan wobbles the least amount.

2 ADD THE WEIGHT. Finally, peel the backing off one of the self-adhesive weight strips and attach it along the centerline of the blade opposite the clip.

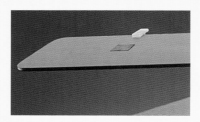

HEATING AND COOLING PROJECTS

3 ATTACH THE FAN. Gain access to the ceiling from above through either the attic or the overhead crawl space. Then position the fan in the hole and secure it to the ceiling joist with nails or screws. Screws tend to hold better over time, as all ceiling fans vibrate and will eventually loosen nails.

Better Fan Support

Most bathroom fans are quite heavy. Couple this with vibration from a spinning fan blade and you have a formula for a sagging fan. Most fans attach to a single ceiling joist—and this often just isn't enough support. A no-sag option that pros look for is a fan with sliding joist braces that secure both sides of the fan in between the ceiling joists, as shown in the drawing below.

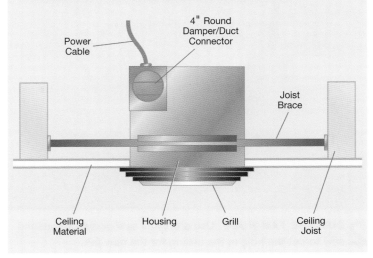

Power Cable

4" Round Damper/Duct Connector

Joist Brace

Ceiling Material

Housing

Grill

Ceiling Joist

4 **CONNECT THE WIRING.** For new installs, you'll have to route new cable to the fan (see pages 149–151). When replacing an existing fan, use the old fan's wiring. Connect the fan wiring to the existing or new wiring with wire nuts, following the manufacturer's wiring diagram. Some units can be fairly complex; in addition to the fan motor, they may have a light and even a night-light to connect.

5 **CONNECT THE DUCTING.** If you're replacing a fan, hook up the existing ducting to the new fan. New installations will need ducting to be installed. See the drawing on page 148 for ducting options. Flexible hose is by far the easiest to run; just be sure to angle the hose down about $\frac{1}{4}$" per foot toward the vent cap so moisture trapped in the hose will run out to the exterior instead of back down into the vent fan.

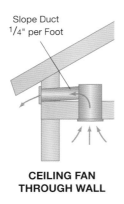

Slope Duct
$1/4$" per Foot

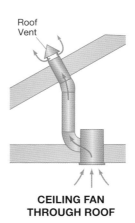

Roof
Vent

**CEILING FAN
THROUGH WALL**

**CEILING FAN
THROUGH ROOF**

6 INSTALL THE MOTOR UNIT. With the fan's wiring complete and the ducting hooked up, you can move back down into the bathroom to complete the job. Insert the fan into the housing and secure it with the screw or screws provided. Plug the wiring harness into the appropriate connector.

7 **ADD THE DIFFUSER AND TRIM.** Install a bulb (if it's a combination fan/light) and the diffuser/trim as shown in the photo above. If you're installing a new fan where there was no fan previously, see below for directions on how to run wiring to your new fan.

Installing new switch wiring

The simplest way to get switch-controlled power to a new fan installation is to tap into the existing light switch for the bathroom. Since you'll need a separate switch for the fan, you can either install a double switch (page 36) in the existing switch box, or enlarge the existing box to hold two switches (as shown here).

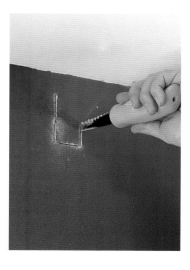

1 **CUT WALL ACCESS.** Start by cutting a hole near the ceiling above the existing switch to access the top plate.

2 **DRILL HOLE IN PLATE FOR WIRING.** Next, drill a hole through the top plate so you can route the wiring from the switch box to the fan.

3 **ENLARGE THE EXISTING SWITCH BOX.** If you're installing a second switch (as shown here), you'll need to enlarge the existing switch box. Use a box as a template to mark the enlarged opening.

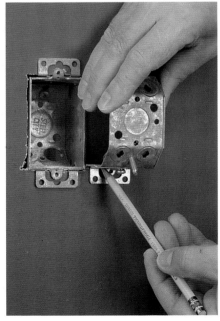

4 **INSTALL THE LARGER BOX.** You can either replace the existing box with a duplex box or, if the existing box is "gangable" (see page 27), attach a second box.

5 **WIRE THE SWITCH.** Route the cable into the box, remove the sheathing, strip the wires, and connect these to the switch (for more on switch wiring, see pages 78–83).

A Programmable Thermostat

A programmable thermostat is one of the best ways to save energy dollars. Simply turning down a thermostat 10 degrees for 8 hours every night can save you 10% a year on your heating costs. Set it lower for an additional 6 hours a day while you're at work and you can save 15%. Programmable thermostats are designed for 24-volt operation. They work with most conventional gas and electrical systems with 2-, 3-, 4-, or 5-wire installations. These will not work with electric baseboard heaters.

Many models come preset with a typical energy-saving program, but it's very easy to custom-program to match your own schedule. Some features to look for in a programmable thermostat are a manual setting that lets you override the program on days where your schedule changes, and a vacation hold. A vacation hold lets the temperature be reset for a prolonged, indefinite period without reprogramming the thermostat.

1 REMOVE THE OLD THERMOSTAT. Begin by turning off power to the furnace at the service panel. Remove the old thermostat's snap-on cover by pulling it straight out. On some thermostats the cover is held in place with screws on the side, which must be loosened first before

you can remove it. Next, note the letters that are printed on the old thermostat's terminals. Then remove one wire at a time and label it to match the terminal letter. Loosen the screws and remove the thermostat from the wall.

2 **MOUNT THE NEW THERMOSTAT.** In most cases, your new thermostat will have two parts: a base and a body. Separate the body from the base, following the manufacturer's instructions. Route the wires through the base. Place a torpedo level on the thermostat and, with

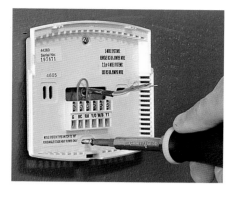

a pencil, transfer the base mounting hole locations to the wall. Drill holes and attach the base to the wall with the screws provided. If you're attaching the unit to drywall, you'll need to use plastic anchors (supplied with most thermostats).

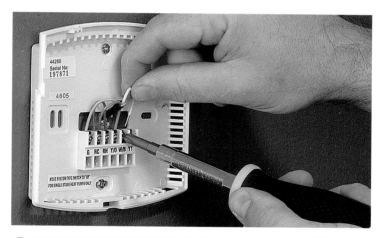

3 **CONNECT THE WIRING.** Make sure that at least ½" of insulation is stripped off the end of each existing wire. Then connect the wires to the thermostat, following the manufacturer's directions; see the drawing on page 155 for typical diagrams. Although you might assume that you simply connect the lettered wires to the corresponding letters on the terminal, this is not so. Make sure to consult the wiring diagrams provided with the thermostat before making any connections.

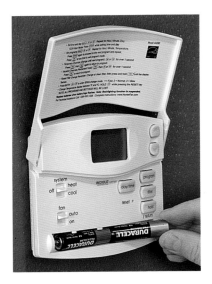

4 INSTALL THE BATTERY BACKUP.

When the wiring is complete, install the backup batteries and attach the body to the base.

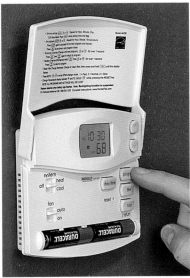

5 PROGRAM THE THERMOSTAT.

Restore power to the furnace and follow the manufacturer's instructions on how to program the thermostat—or use the pre-programmed settings. Programming varies in complexity: There are simple thermostats that use the same time and temperature settings, which you program in for every day of the week, up to advanced units where each day of the week can be programmed separately. More common are models with separate programming cycles for the weekdays and one or two cycles for the weekend. Typical thermostats let you program four different periods per day—for waking, leaving, returning, and sleeping.

4-Wire Heat/Cool System

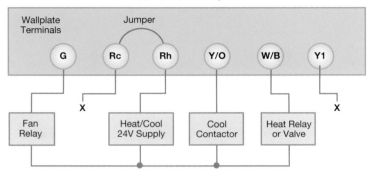

5-Wire Heat/Cool System

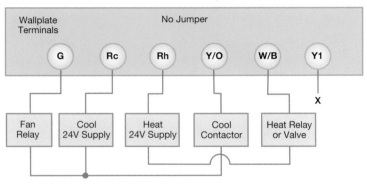

Single-Stage Heat Pump System

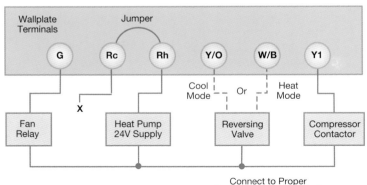

A Programmable Thermostat   **155**

7

Home Electronics

IN DAYS OF TECHNOLOGY INNOCENCE past, only professionals could extend a phone line, run a cable TV cable, or link computers into a network. That's because only pros had access to the specialized parts needed. Today, though, with electronics so much a part of everyday life, savvy companies offer do-it-yourself-friendly parts so that the rest of us can handle these projects and more.

Extending a Phone Line

Prior to the 1960's phones were "hard-wired" directly to a telephone jack. If you wanted to change the phone, move it, or extend it, you called the phone company. Now phones are equipped with modular jacks that can be plugged and unplugged as easily as a lamp. And with the do-it-yourself-friendly parts that are readily available at home centers and hardware stores, anyone can easily move and extend phone lines.

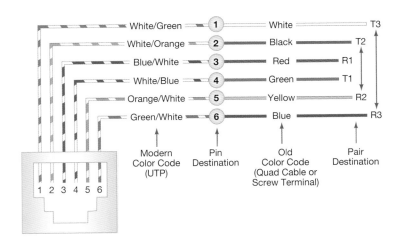

Modern Color Code (UTP)	Pin Destination	Old Color Code (Quad Cable or Screw Terminal)	Pair Destination
White/Green	1	White	T3
White/Orange	2	Black	T2
Blue/White	3	Red	R1
White/Blue	4	Green	T1
Orange/White	5	Yellow	R2
Green/White	6	Blue	R3

QUICK FIX

Splitters and Splices

Want to quickly extend or share a phone line? Use one of the many splitters and splices available. These accessories all sport modular plugs and connectors for quick and easy modifications.

TELEPHONE CABLE AND CONNECTORS. There are two types of telephone cable: flat line cord, which terminates with modular plugs, and "station wire," a multi-conductor, plastic-sheathed cable that routes lines from your home's interface jack to the rooms throughout your home. Older

station wire housed four conductors; newer wire houses six. Although the color codes are different, the function of the wires is the same (drawing on page 158). The "T" designator stands for "tip," and the "R" stands for "ring." A single phone line requires one pair of tip and ring wires. Old station wire can carry two separate lines; new wire can handle three. Telephone jacks may be flush-mounted to an electrical box, or surface-mounted.

INSTALLING A FLUSH-MOUNTED JACK. Phone lines in newer homes terminate in a flush-mounted jack. These can attach to an existing box or a newly installed remodel or "cut-in" box (pages 74–75). The screw terminals on most jacks are color-coded to make connecting the new phone line a snap. (For old/new wire color equivalents, see the drawing on page 158.)

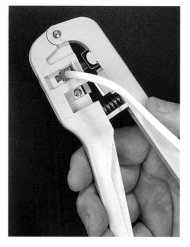

ATTACHING MODULAR PLUGS. Inexpensive modular-plug crimping tools (like the one shown here) are readily available and make quick work of attaching plugs onto flat line cord.

Installing a surface-mounted jack

If you don't want to bother with cutting in a box for a phone line and routing the cable through a wall, you can install a surface-mounted jack.

1 SECURE THE JACK TO THE WALL. Surface-mounted jacks can be attached either to trim or to walls. To attach a jack to trim, mark the mounting hole locations on the trim, drill pilot holes, and attach the jack with screws. For wall coverings like drywall (which offers no purchase for screws), it's best to use plastic anchors to secure the jack to the wall.

2 CONNECT THE PHONE WIRE. To connect a phone cable, remove 1½" of sheathing and strip the wires. Loosen the terminal screws on the jack (the ones shown here are color-coded), wrap the wires around the screws, and tighten. Then snap on the cover to conceal the wiring.

P R O T I P

Cable Staplers

Although it looks like an ordinary stapler, the tip of a cable stapler is notched to fit over cable. The staples are likewise shaped. Pros use these to quickly staple cable in place, since the staple straddles the cable and can't damage it as the staple is driven into the wall or trim.

Routing exterior phone wire

Instead of cutting into your interior walls to run telephone wire, pros often run the cable on the exterior of the home. They'll drill through a wall at the desired location and feed the wire into the room, where it terminates in a surface-mounted or flush-mounted jack.

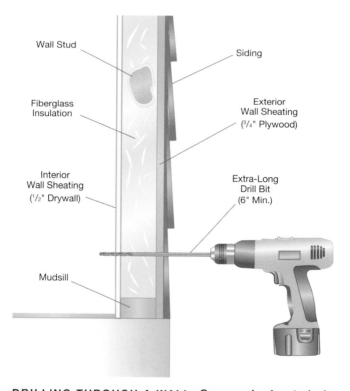

Wall Stud

Siding

Fiberglass Insulation

Exterior Wall Sheating ($^3/_4$" Plywood)

Interior Wall Sheating ($^1/_2$" Drywall)

Extra-Long Drill Bit (6" Min.)

Mudsill

DRILLING THROUGH A WALL. Once you've located where you want the new or extended line in your home, the first thing to do is locate the studs with a stud finder. The second item: Verify that there are no electrical, plumbing, gas, or heating/cooling lines in the wall. Pros use extra-long drill bits for drilling through a wall, but you can also use an extension to lengthen a bit. Drill the smallest hole needed, and after you've fished the wire through the wall (see page 162), make sure to seal around the hole on both sides of the wall with 100% silicone caulk.

Fishing with a
Soda Straw

Phone wire is flexible, so it's difficult to fish it through a wall. Although you could use a fish tape for this (if the hooked end is small enough to fit in the wall holes), another solution is to insert a plastic straw through the holes and fish the wire through the straw.

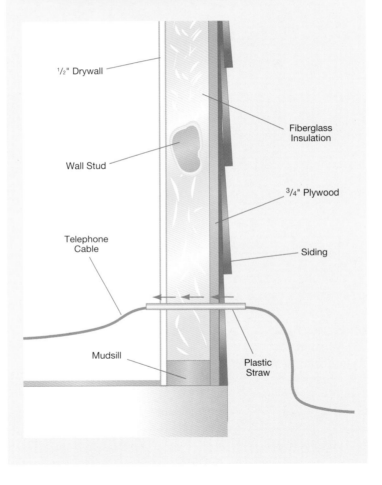

½" Drywall

Fiberglass
Insulation

Wall Stud

¾" Plywood

Telephone
Cable

Siding

Mudsill

Plastic
Straw

Extending a Cable-TV Cable

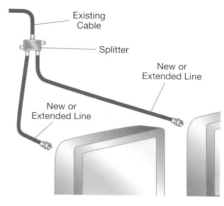

The lifeline that keeps entertainment flowing into and through most homes is coaxial cable, whether it's used for cable or satellite TV. Coaxial cable has an inner conductor to carry the signal, an inner core to protect the inner conductor, a braided shield over the inner core to prevent interference, and exterior sheathing, usually black. Two common types of coaxial cable are RG-59 and RG-6. RG-59 is used for most cable TV circuits. RG-6, with its thicker inner conductor and heavier shielding, is used for satellite TV systems. Typically, a main line is attached to a splitter, where multiple lines can be run to separate locations (drawing above).

Existing Cable

Splitter

New or Extended Line

New or Extended Line

F-CONNECTORS. The male and female connectors used with coaxial cable are called F-connectors; they feature screw threads on their ends for quick and secure connections. The outer case of the F-connector attaches to the cable's shielding to ensure continuous shielding of the inner conductor. F-connectors may be single units that thread on or crimp on, or two-piece units that use a ring to crimp the shielding firmly against the connector.

Working with F-connectors

Although you can attach F-connectors to coaxial cable without a coaxial stripper and crimper, consider purchasing these inexpensive specialty tools. They do such an excellent job of creating reliable, interference-free connections that most folks feel the cost is worth it.

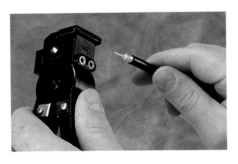

1 PREPARE THE CABLE. To install an F-connector, you'll first need to prepare the cable. If you're using a coaxial stripper (as shown here), simply insert the end of the cable in the stripper, press the jaws together, and pivot the tool around the cable a few times to cut away the exact amount of sheathing, shielding, and inner core. To do this manually, remove ½" of the sheathing, taking care not to cut into the delicate shielding. Then remove ⅜" of the inner core (a coaxial stripper will do both of these operations simultaneously without damage).

PRO TIP

Wall-Mounted F-Connectors

Although you can run coaxial cable directly out of a wall or box, pros typically terminate the cable at the box and install a flush-mounted F-connector.

2 SLIP ON THE CRIMPING RING. If you're using a two-piece F-connector (connector plus crimping ring), your next step is to slip the crimping ring over the outer sheathing of the cable.

3 FOLD BACK THE SHIELD. To create the best possible connection between the connector and the shielding, peel the shielding away from the inner core and fold it back over the core, as shown.

4 PRESS THE CONNECTOR IN PLACE. Now you can press the connector over the prepared end of the cable. Push until the inner core butts fully up against its stop inside the connector.

5 CRIMP THE CONNECTOR. Crimping the connector actually crushes the shielding against the connector to ensure a reliable connection. You can do this with locking-jaw pliers or standard pliers, but you'll achieve a better connection if you use a cable crimper, as shown here.

HOME ELECTRONICS

Networking Computers

Homes with multiple computers or home offices often need to hook up or "network" computers together to share data, or peripherals like printers or media backup devices. Networking is also commonly used to link multiple computers to a single high-speed Internet access point for sharing access. Single-point Internet access is usually as simple as plugging a computer into a standard phone line.

Cable options

There are three cable options to choose from to network computers: CAT-5 cable (see page 167), coaxial cable (RG-58), and no-cable or wireless networking (see page 167). Of these three, CAT-5 and wireless are the most prevalent in homes. RG-58, or "thinnet," is used mainly in large commercial business.

A SIMPLE NETWORK. To share a common peripheral or to join computers together to share data, cable is run from each computer to a common hub (drawing at right). A hub is basically an electronic postman that delivers data (mail) to different computers (homes). Each computer must be either pre-wired for this or have a network interface card to allow networking. Older computers that require an interface card may also need separate software called a "driver" to access the card and allow the computer to communicate with the hub.

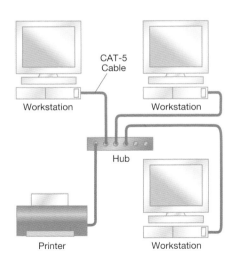

CAT-5 Cable

Workstation

Workstation

Hub

Printer

Workstation

CAT-5 WIRING AND CONNECTORS. Category-5 cable consists of four twisted pairs of conductors sheathed in flexible plastic. The cable can be rated for interior or exterior use. Connections are made via 8-pin modular plugs and jacks, commonly referred to as "Ethernet" connections when used for computers. Shown in the top photo are two different-length "patch" cords—cords that have modular connectors at both ends, and a flush-mounted wall plate that can accept up to four separate (RJ-45) jacks.

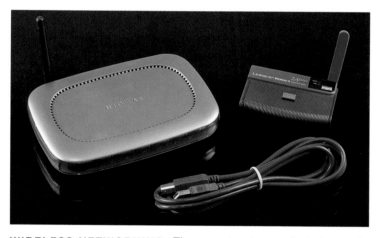

WIRELESS NETWORKING. There are two types of wireless networks: a hardware-access point network, which requires a central device to distribute data, and an ad-hoc or peer-to-peer network which uses wi-fi (wireless-fidelity) technology. The central device in a hardware-access point network is called a router (left in photo above). If the router is being used to share a high-speed or DSL Internet line with other computers, the Internet will hook up to the router so it can share its connection with other computers. Each of these computers will need a wireless hub to "catch" the data (right in photo).

⚠ WARNING

• Read and understand instruction manual before use.
• Do not use in or near live circuits. Steel tapes are conductive, nylon tape has a metal tip.
• Disconnect power before working.
• Do not exceed maximum pull force. Tape may break. Failure to observe these warnings may result in severe injury or death.

• Keep secure footing.
• Do not open case when tape is coiled, tape is stored under tension.
• Do not use pliers or other tools to pull tape. Do not force a pull that is hung up.

DECAL NO. 500 2548 0

8

Adding and Extending Circuits

M AKE NO MISTAKE: Adding or extending a circuit is potentially a big deal. With care, though, you can take on this job safely and successfully, as long as you have some basic knowledge of how wiring is run throughout a house. In this chapter, we'll show you how to extend an existing circuit with surface-mounted wiring and via baseboards—and how to add a completely new circuit.

Surface-Mounted Wiring

Want to add a ceiling light and switch but don't want to cut holes in your walls? Consider surface-mounted wiring. Surface-mounted wiring "taps" into an existing circuit; then you run the wiring in plastic or metal raceway (like protective "tubing") that attaches directly to a wall or ceiling. Raceway is available in a variety of pre-cut lengths, or you can cut it to a custom length with a hacksaw. Connectors, elbows, and boxes complete the run (see page 43). Then you run wire and hook up the new fixtures.

(see page 43)

PRO TIP

Metal Versus Plastic Raceway

You can buy surface-mounted parts and raceway in either metal or plastic. Although the metal type isn't as easy to work with as plastic, it stands up better over time and is the choice of most professionals. Note: Both types are paintable, and when painted the same color as the wall, will almost disappear.

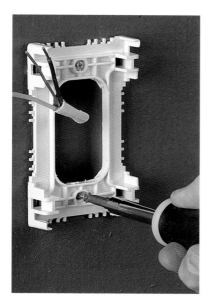

1 CONVERT THE EXISTING BOX.

Locate the receptacle that's closest to where you want your new wiring. Turn off the power to the receptacle at the breaker or fuse panel. Remove the old cover plate and receptacle. Then attach a "starter" box to the electrical box. The base or mounting plate of the two-part starter box has a large rectangular hole in it to let the wiring pass through into the new box. Screw the base to the electrical box as shown.

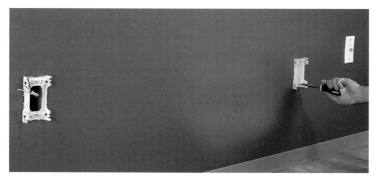

2 LOCATE AND INSTALL NEW MOUNTING PLATE.

Surface-mounted boxes are attached to the wall by either screwing into studs or drilling holes for plastic anchors. To use plastic anchors, position the plate of the box where you want it and make a mark through the mounting holes in the back. Then drill holes, insert the plastic anchors, and screw the plate to the wall.

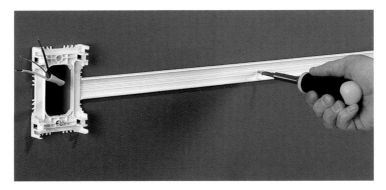

3 **INSTALL THE RACEWAY.** Next, measure and cut raceway to reach the new box (or boxes). Press-fit connectors, and inside and outside elbows, make this an easy task. Just make sure to subtract the length of the connector from the raceway before you cut it to length. Attach the raceway to the wall by screwing directly into studs, or drill holes for the plastic anchors provided.

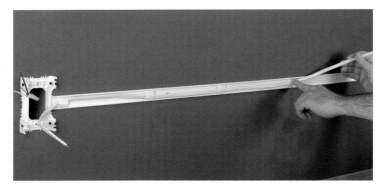

4 **RUN THE WIRING.** Running wire through surface-mounted raceways is very simple. Just cut the wire to length plus 6" extra on each end for your electrical connections. Then place it in the raceway and thread the ends into the boxes. Most surface-mounted systems come with snap-in, flexible plastic clips that fit inside the track to hold the wiring in place.

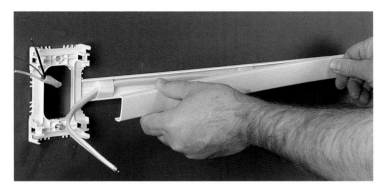

5 **ATTACH THE RACEWAY COVER.** With the wiring in place, you can install the cover(s) onto the raceway to conceal and protect the wiring. Both the metal and plastic varieties simply snap onto the raceway.

6 **ATTACH BOX TO ORIGINAL RECEPTACLE.** After you've installed all the covers on the raceways, you can add the box to the mounting plate. With plastic parts, the box simply snaps over the mounting plate. With metal parts, the cover secures to the mounting plate with screws.

7 **CONNECT THE WIRING AT THE ORIGINAL BOX.** With the box in place, you can make your electrical connections. If you tapped into an existing receptacle (as shown here), you'll need to wire the receptacle as a middle-of-run receptacle (for more on this, see pages 84–86).

8 **INSTALL THE ORIGINAL RECEPTACLE.** Once wired, gently push the wiring into the surface-mounted box and secure the receptacle to the box with the receptacle's mounting screws.

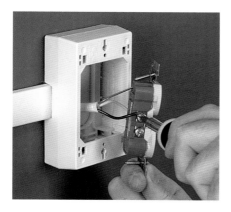

9 CONNECT WIRING AT NEW BOX. At the new box (or boxes), strip the ends of the wires you've run as needed to make your electrical connections. For receptacle wiring, see pages 84–86. For switch wiring, see pages 78–83.

10 INSTALL NEW SWITCH OR RECEPTACLE. Push the wiring gently into the surface-mounted boxes and secure the switch or receptacle to the box. Finally, you can add any cover plates to the surface-mounted boxes as shown in the photo above. Note: If you've installed metal raceways, you may need to secure the raceways to the wall with metal straps that fit over the raceway. In most cases, you'll need to secure these to the wall with plastic anchors.

ADDING AND EXTENDING CIRCUITS

Extending a Circuit via Baseboards

Extending a circuit doesn't always mean cutting access holes in walls and running cables through basements or ceilings. If your home has baseboards (or you'd consider putting them in), you can use the method described here to route a cable behind baseboards that cover your work, making it virtually invisible.

There are a couple of things to do before you can extend a circuit. First, locate an existing box that you feel is a good candidate for extension. Either middle-of-run or end-of-run receptacles (pages 84–86) will work fine, as long as they're not controlled by a switch. Second, check the circuit breaker to make sure it can handle the additional load.

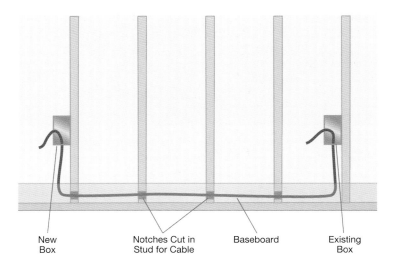

New
Box

Notches Cut in
Stud for Cable

Baseboard

Existing
Box

1 REMOVE THE BASEBOARDS. Once you've identified the receptacle you're going to extend, turn off the power and tag the main panel. Then remove the cover plate and the receptacle mounting screws. Loosen the screw terminals, disconnect the wires, and set the receptacle aside. Then remove the baseboard or molding with a prybar or stiff-blade putty knife; slip a wide putty knife behind the prybar to prevent damaging the wall covering.

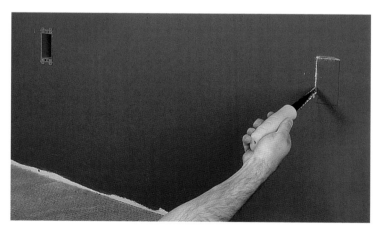

2 CUT THE NEW BOX HOLE. Determine the location of the new electrical box (see page 72 for recommended box heights for switches and receptacles). Locate the wall studs with an electronic stud finder, mark the box outline on the wall, and cut the hole with a drywall saw.

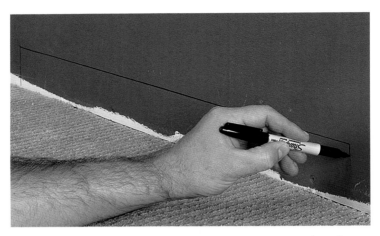

3 MARK THE EXTENSION NOTCH. The next step is to lay out the notch behind the baseboards where you'll run the new cable. First, measure the height of your baseboard and subtract 1/2" from this to determine the height of the notch. Locate the studs with an electronic stud finder and identify the start and stop points of the notch; draw the outline of the notch directly on the wall covering.

4 CUT THE NOTCH. Use a drywall saw to cut most of the notch outline. When you hit a stud, switch to a utility knife and carefully cut through the drywall. Lift out the waste and set it aside; you'll use it later to patch the extension notch.

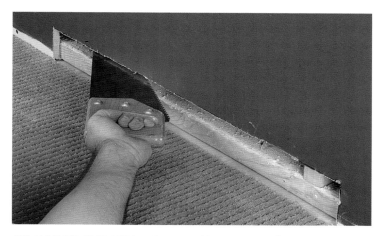

5 **NOTCH THE WALL STUDS.** Now you need to cut notches at the bottom of each wall stud for the new cable. The notches should be just deep enough to accept the cable (roughly ½" deep). The simplest way to cut the notches is to define the top and bottom of the notch with a handsaw (as shown here). Then use a chisel and hammer to knock out the waste. Check each notch with a piece of cable to make sure it's deep enough.

6 **RUN THE CABLE.** Now feed the cable from the existing box hole to the new box hole by threading it down the walls to the extension notch in the wall covering and through the notches in the studs.

7 **ATTACH METAL COVER PLATES.** If the baseboard for the room is nailed in place—and even if it's not—it's a good idea to protect the cable from possible damage by nailing on metal cover plates as illustrated here.

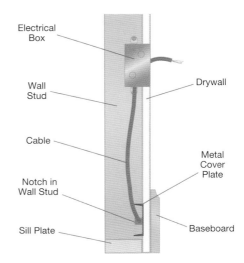

Electrical Box

Wall Stud

Cable

Notch in Wall Stud

Sill Plate

Drywall

Metal Cover Plate

Baseboard

Cross Section

8 **PATCH THE DRYWALL.** If you saved the waste from the extension notch, you can use this for a quick and easy patch job. Insert the waste in the notch and secure it to the sole plate and studs with drywall screws. Cover any screw heads and fill any gaps with spackling compound.

9 CONNECT THE WIRING. At each box hole, thread the cable through the box and secure the box to the wall covering (pages 74–75). Then connect the receptacles or switches. For receptacle wiring, see pages 84–86; for switch wiring, see pages 78–83.

10 RE-INSTALL THE BASE-BOARDS. All that's left is to replace the baseboards. If you're reusing the baseboard, pull the old nails out from the back of the molding with a pair of locking-jaw pliers. Don't pound them back out the front, or you'll splinter the face of the molding. Reposition the old baseboard and secure it with 2" casing nails driven into the sole plate and wall studs. Fill any nail holes and touch up with paint if necessary.

ADDING AND EXTENDING CIRCUITS

Adding a Circuit

Adding a new circuit to a home is a major job: You need to install a new breaker in the service panel, and run new cable up and down walls and through a basement, crawl space, or attic. First, you must be sure your service panel can handle another circuit. If the service panel has any empty breaker slots, odds are that you're good to go. Even if all your slots are full, you can often replace an existing single breaker with a split breaker (page 41) to access additional power. If you're not sure your existing panel can handle another circuit, check with a licensed electrician or your local building inspector.

Before you tackle adding a circuit, you must follow the electrical code and have all your planned work approved by a local building inspector. You'll also need a working knowledge of basic carpentry—especially framing. It's critical that you understand how your house is put together before you start drilling holes in it. The circuit we added here was a separate 20-amp GFCI receptacle to power a jetted tub (drawing below).

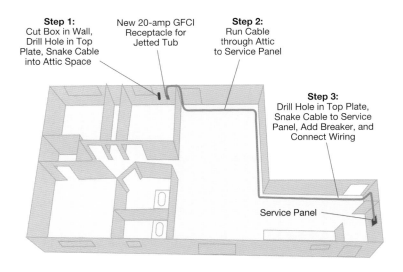

Step 1:
Cut Box in Wall, Drill Hole in Top Plate, Snake Cable into Attic Space

New 20-amp GFCI Receptacle for Jetted Tub

Step 2:
Run Cable through Attic to Service Panel

Step 3:
Drill Hole in Top Plate, Snake Cable to Service Panel, Add Breaker, and Connect Wiring

Service Panel

1 **RUN CABLE TO THE PANEL.** Turn off the main breaker. (Note: The main power lines into the panel will still be live.) Then remove the panel screws and cover. Locate a knockout inside the panel and remove it to allow for fishing the cable. Extend a fish tape up through the knockout and into the ceiling. Attach the new cable and pull the cable down into the panel. Leave yourself about 24" of excess for connecting to the breaker later.

2 **CUT ACCESS HOLE IN NEW LOCATION.** At the new circuit location, cut a hole near the ceiling or floor to access either the top plate or the sole plate (depending on whether you'll route the cable through the attic or the basement).

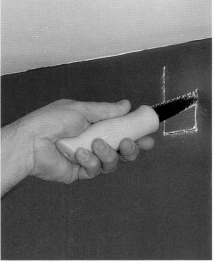

3 **DRILL HOLE IN PLATE AT NEW LOCATION.** Before you drill a hole in the top plate or sole plate, check the area where you'll be drilling to make sure there are no obstructions, plumbing, or gas or electrical lines near it. Use an extra-long drill bit or a bit fitted with an extension to drill through the plate. Center the bit on the plate and hold the drill at an angle as you drill, to keep from damaging the wall covering.

4 **PULL CABLE TO NEW LOCATION.** With the hole drilled in the plate, you can begin fishing the cable. Start routing the new cable from the service panel to the new location, whether in the attic or basement. Then feed the fish tape through the hole in the plate and into the new location. Attach the cable to the fish tape and pull the cable through the plate.

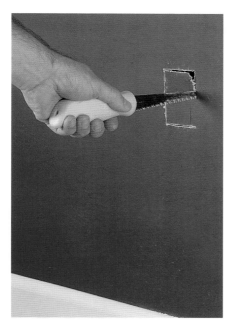

5 **CUT THE NEW BOX HOLE.** At the new location, determine the position of the new box or boxes (see page 72 for recommended box heights). Locate the wall studs with an electronic stud finder, and position the box to one side of the studs. Trace around the box and cut out the waste with a drywall saw.

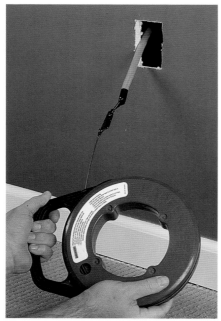

6 **FISH THE CABLE TO THE NEW BOX.** Run a fish tape from the access hole into the newly cut box. Attach the cable to the fish tape and pull it down through the new box hole.

7 **INSTALL THE NEW BOX.** Disconnect the cable from the fish tape and feed it through the access hole for the new receptacle box. As always, make sure to leave yourself plenty of excess cable. Insert the cable into the box (if necessary), secure it with the cable clamp, and install the box in the wall.

8 **CONNECT THE CABLE AT NEW LOCATION.** Remove the sheathing from the cable, strip the wires, and connect them to your new switch or receptacle. See pages 84–86 for receptacle wiring and pages 78–83 for switch wiring. Press each receptacle or switch gently into its box and secure with mounting screws; add the cover plate(s).

9 **ADD BREAKER TO SERVICE PANEL.** Back at the service panel, make sure the main breaker is off and tag it. Even with the main breaker off, there's still power in the box at the main leads—take care to work safely here (see pages 60–61). Then insert the new breaker. If you're replacing a single breaker with a split breaker, first disconnect the black "hot" wire going to the existing breaker; then remove the old breaker and install the split breaker.

10 **CONNECT CABLE TO THE BREAKER.** To connect your new cable to the new breaker, first strip off about 16" to 18" of sheathing. Route the white wire neatly over to the neutral bus; do the same for the bare ground wire. Strip $\frac{1}{2}$" of insulation off the white wire and connect it to the neutral bus. Loosen an unused screw on the bus, slide the wire under the screw, and tighten. Then neatly route the hot black wire to the new breaker. Strip off $\frac{1}{2}$" of insulation; loosen the terminal screw, slip the wire under the screw, and tighten. Restore power and test the new circuit.

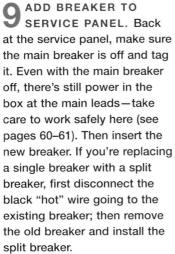

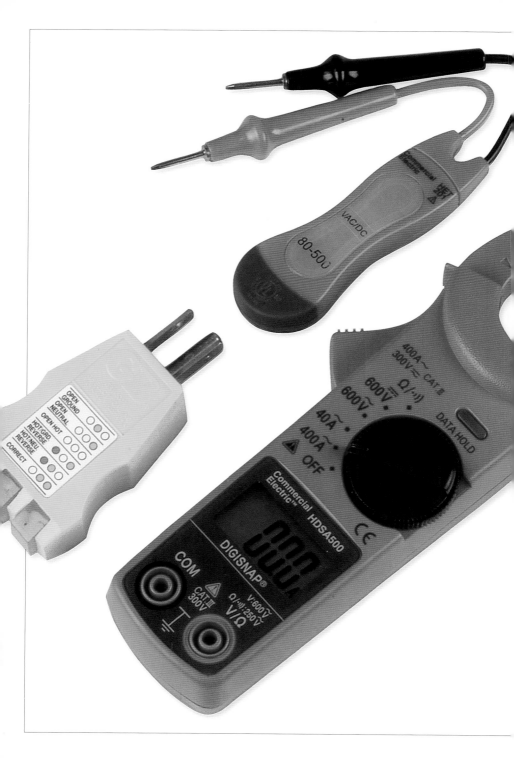

Troubleshooting Electrical Circuits

WHEN THE LIGHTS GO OUT, you shouldn't be left in the dark. Since the rules governing electricity are very straightforward, there's a logical strategy to finding the cause when electrical circuits fail. In this chapter, we'll put this strategy to use with electrical testers, checking out everything from the service panel through the branch circuits to the lamp that left you in the dark.

Using Electrical Testers

Electrical testers are like X-ray eyes that let you "see" what's happening in a circuit. The four most common testers: a circuit tester, a continuity tester, a receptacle analyzer, and a multi-meter.

CIRCUIT TESTER. A circuit tester (often called a neon tester) is a pair of probes hooked up to a neon bulb that will light when 120 volts passes through it. To use one, insert the probes into a receptacle as shown. If the lamp lights, power is present. You can also touch the black (ground) lead to the ground lug of a receptacle or switch and touch the red lead to the screw terminals; the lamp will light when you find the "hot" wire.

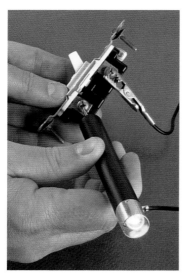

CONTINUITY TESTER. A continuity tester detects a continuous path for current. It's just a pair of probes, a lamp, and a battery. If you touch the probes together, the lamp will light, telling you that the path is continuous. A continuity tester should only be used with the power off. (See pages 202–203 for a common use of a continuity tester.)

Open Ground	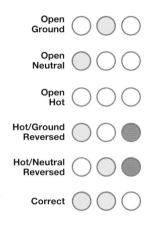	
Open Neutral		
Open Hot		
Hot/Ground Reversed		
Hot/Neutral Reversed		
Correct		

RECEPTACLE ANALYZER.
A favored diagnostic tool of pros, a receptacle analyzer will tell you the condition of a receptacle at a glance. To use one, just plug it into a receptacle. Most analyzers have three lamps built into the end that light up in various combinations to describe what's going on in the receptacle.

The six most common lamp combinations are illustrated in the drawing above. They indicate if the ground, neutral, or hot side is open, if the hot and ground lines are reversed, if the hot and neutral lines are reversed, or if the receptacle is wired correctly. That's a whole lot of information to get without even removing a cover plate.

TROUBLESHOOTING ELECTRICAL CIRCUITS

**USING A MULTI-
METER.** Multi-meters
come in two flavors:
analog and digital. Both
use probes (or test leads)
to measure current,
voltage, and resistance.
An analog multi-meter
(top photo) uses a single
pivoting indicator and a
fairly complex scale to
display a measurement; a
digital multi-meter (see
page 200) sports an easy-
to-read digital display.

**MEASURING RESIST-
ANCE OR CONTINUITY.**
Flip the function switch
to resistance (or ohms,
identified by the omega
symbol). Touch the test
leads to the device. A
zero reading or audible
tone indicates continuity.
Any other display is the
resistance in ohms. On a
digital meter, an "OL"
reading indicates infinite
resistance or an "open."

MEASURING VOLTAGE.
Turn the function switch
to AC or DC voltage.
Touch the probes to the
device and read the dis-
play. (Note: Inexpensive
analog meters can't accu-
rately read AC voltage.)

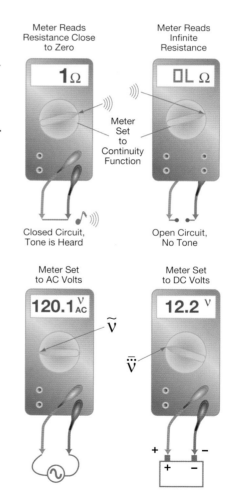

Meter Reads
Resistance Close
to Zero

Meter Reads
Infinite
Resistance

Meter
Set
to
Continuity
Function

Closed Circuit,
Tone is Heard

Open Circuit,
No Tone

Meter Set
to AC Volts

Meter Set
to DC Volts

MEASURING CURRENT.
To measure current, you need to temporarily "break" the circuit (remove a wire from a receptacle or switch) and insert the meter into the circuit. This lets circuit current flow through the meter so it can measure it (alternatively, use the amp probe described on page 57 to measure current without disturbing the circuit). Select AC or DC amps and turn off power. Break the circuit and connect the test leads; restore power and make your measurement. (Most inexpensive analog meters can't accurately measure AC current.)

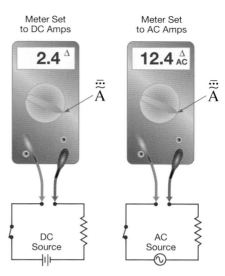

Meter Set to DC Amps

Meter Set to AC Amps

Step 1: Turn Off Power
Step 2: Break Circuit
Step 3: Insert Meter
Step 4: Turn On Power and Test

Clamp-On Test Leads

Pros typically carry an assortment of specialty tips that screw on or press onto the ends of their test leads. The most common of these are clamping tips or "alligator" clips. These serve as the much-needed third or fourth hand while making measurements. Often, the meter is held in one hand while the other hand selects function and range. This leaves no hands free to hold the test leads—alligator clips to the rescue.

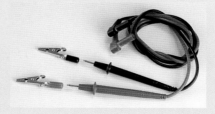

No Power

You're enjoying your favorite TV show and suddenly the lights go out. What to do? First, don't panic. Second, grab your electrical emergency kit (see the sidebar below) and start troubleshooting.

LOCALIZE THE PROBLEM. Your first step is to determine the extent of the power outage. If you notice that your entire home is dark, look outside at your neighbors' homes. If they're dark, too, odds are it's the power company; give them  a call to see what's up. If the outage appears to be affecting just your home, try flipping on various lights to identify which rooms are affected. If power is out only to a specific device (a TV or appliance), check to make sure it's plugged in, someone hasn't flipped a switch, or the bulb hasn't simply burned out.

Electrical Emergency Kit

The Boy Scout motto "Be Prepared" really applies to electrical emergencies. One way to be prepared for emergencies is to have a repair kit located in an easily accessible place. Items to include in the kit: a flashlight with spare bulb and batteries, electrical testers (a digital multi-meter is your best bet), spare fuses or  breakers, hand tools (see Chapter 3), and replacement parts (receptacles, switches, etc.). Finally, copy the power company's phone number onto a piece of tape and attach this to the inside lid of your kit.

CHECK THE MAIN BREAKER. If power is out house-wide, check the main breaker to see whether it has tripped. If you know that power is out only to a portion of your home, it's most likely a blown fuse or tripped breaker. Check your fuses or breakers, and replace or reset them as needed (see pages 200–201 for more on this).

TEST FOR POWER WITH A METER. If the main breaker isn't tripped and you still have no power, check to see if you've got power coming into the house. Remove the service panel cover screws and set the cover aside. Then use a multi-meter to check for incoming power. Place one test probe on each of the main hot lines coming into the panel, as shown here. If power is OK, your meter will display 220 to 240 volts. No power reading means that it's the power company.

Troubleshooting Switches

When you flip on a light switch and nothing happens, most of the time it's just the bulb or bulbs. Occasionally, it's the fuse or breaker of the branch circuit. But sometimes it's the switch itself, because all switches eventually wear out. There are two methods to identify a bad switch: out-of-circuit and in-circuit (see the sidebar on page 197).

Out-of-circuit testing

To check a switch out of circuit, remove the switch and use a continuity tester or multi-meter to test the switch.

1 REMOVE THE SWITCH. Turn off power to the switch and remove the cover plate. Remove the switch mounting screws, and gently pull it out of the box. Then loosen the screw terminals and remove the wires.

2 CHECKING A SINGLE-POLE SWITCH. Touch the probes of a continuity tester or multi-meter (set to read resistance) to the screw terminals of the switch (drawing at right). Flip the switch and observe the tester's light or the meter's display. One position should read zero, the other infinite. The lamp of the continuity tester should go on and off.

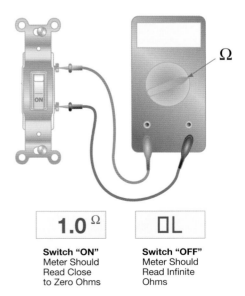

1.0 Ω

Switch "ON"
Meter Should
Read Close
to Zero Ohms

OL

Switch "OFF"
Meter Should
Read Infinite
Ohms

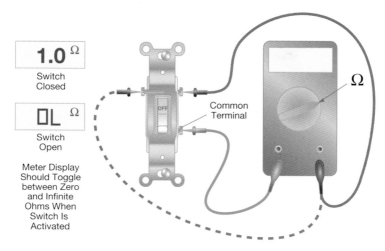

1.0 Ω
Switch
Closed

OL Ω
Switch
Open

Meter Display
Should Toggle
between Zero
and Infinite
Ohms When
Switch Is
Activated

Common
Terminal

Ω

3 **CHECKING A 3-WAY SWITCH.** Press the black meter lead against the black common terminal. Touch the red test lead in turn against each of the traveler screws and observe the display.

In-Circuit Switch Testing

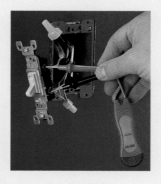

Electricians often test a switch in circuit with the power on, to save time. After removing the cover plate and switch mounting screws, they pull the switch out of the box. (**Safety note:** Extra care is required here, as power is present on the switch terminals; see pages 60–61 for working safely with electricity.) The exposed screw terminals are touched with the probes of a circuit tester or multi-meter. With a circuit tester, the lamp should go on and off when the switch is toggled. With a multi-meter, the display will toggle between 120 and 0 volts when a good switch is toggled. A bad switch will read either 120 or 0 volts regardless of the switch position.

TROUBLESHOOTING ELECTRICAL CIRCUITS

Troubleshooting Receptacles

If you've localized a power outage down to a single receptacle, you can check the receptacle either in circuit or out of circuit.

IN-CIRCUIT TESTING. One way to check a receptacle is to plug in a known good device, like a nearby lamp. But this will only tell you whether it's working properly or not. It won't tell you the condition of the receptacle. A receptacle analyzer, though, will give you an instant snapshot of the unit's condition. The lamps on the end of the analyzer will identify any problems; see page 191 for standard lamp codes.

Out-of-circuit testing

To test a receptacle out of circuit, you'll need to secure power to the receptacle, remove it, and check it with a continuity tester or multi-meter. Note that this test will only identify whether the receptacle is good or not; it doesn't check the wiring.

1 **REMOVE THE RECEPTACLE.** Locate the appropriate fuse or breaker to secure power to the receptacle. Remove the cover plate and mounting screws, and gently pull the receptacle from the box. Loosen the screw terminals and remove the wires.

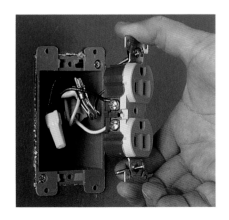

2 **TEST CONTINUITY.** To check a receptacle with a continuity tester or multi-meter (set to resistance), insert the test probes into the hot and neutral slots, as shown in the drawing at right. The lamp on the continuity tester should not light, and the meter should read infinite resistance (OL on a digital meter). Move one lead to the ground lug and the other first to the neutral and then to the hot slot; the continuity tester should not light, and the meter should read infinite resistance. Readings other than this indicate that the receptacle is bad.

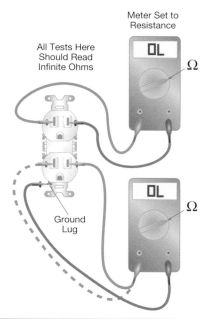

Meter Set to Resistance

All Tests Here Should Read Infinite Ohms

Ground Lug

One-Half of Receptacle Is Dead

If you encounter a receptacle where only one-half of the receptacle is dead, check the links between the terminal screws on the sides of the receptacle (see page 85). One or more of these links are removed to create a switch-controlled receptacle or to separate the halves of the receptacle. You can quickly check the condition of the links by touching the probes of a continuity tester or multi-meter (set to read resistance) across the terminals. A lighted lamp or zero resistance indicates a good link.

TROUBLESHOOTING ELECTRICAL CIRCUITS

Testing Fuses

When a fuse blows, it may or may not give a visual indication that is has blown. Frequently, a fuse can appear perfectly normal but be bad. Don't trust your eyes when it comes to checking fuses. Instead, use a continuity tester or multi-meter set to read resistance. Both cartridge and screw-in fuses are tested in the same way.

CHECKING A CARTRIDGE FUSE. It's easy to check a cartridge fuse. Set the fuse on a work surface and press the probes of a continuity tester or multi-meter to each of the fuse's metal end caps, as shown. On a good fuse, the lamp will light or the meter will read low resistance (anywhere from 0 to 75 ohms, depending on the type and size of the fuse). A bad or "open" fuse will not allow the lamp to light and will display infinite resistance on a meter.

CHECKING A SCREW-IN OR PLUG FUSE. Screw-in and plug fuses are tested the same way as cartridge fuses; the only challenge is pressing the probes against the fuse to get a good reading. One probe is pressed against the metal point at the bottom of the fuse; the other is pressed against the metal threads, as shown in the photo above. On a tamper-proof fuse (page 42), press the second lead to the metal spring located at the top of the plastic threads.

Testing Breakers

When too much current flows through a breaker, a bimetal strip inside heats up and bends until a spring-loaded contact opens or "trips" to cut off current. A tripped breaker can be identified in two ways: The on/off lever is halfway between off and on, or the built-in indicator (usually red or orange) is showing. To reset a breaker, flip the lever to the OFF position and then toggle it to the ON position.

IN-CIRCUIT TEST. Set a multi-meter to read AC volts. Connect its black (ground) lead to the service panel's ground or metal case; touch the red lead to the breaker's hot screw terminal, as shown. On a good breaker in the ON position, the meter will display 120 volts; in the OFF position, 0 volts. A bad breaker reads 120 or 0 volts in both positions.

OUT-OF-CIRCUIT TEST. Turn off main power, disconnect the hot wire, and remove the breaker. Set a multi-meter to read resistance. Press the leads against the breaker's metal connection tabs. The meter display should shift between zero and infinite ohms as you toggle the breaker; if it doesn't, it's bad.

Testing a Lamp

The electrical parts of a lamp are few: a plug and power cord, a switch, and a socket with bulb (see page 128). This makes troubleshooting a straightforward process of elimination.

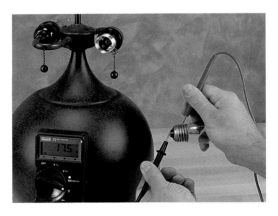

1 TEST THE BULB. Although it may seem obvious, it's always best to make sure your lamp's bulb or bulbs are good (frequently, they appear perfectly fine but have burned out near the base and you can't see this). Use a multi-meter or continuity tester to make sure the filament is intact. A good bulb will have low resistance (0 to 50 ohms); a bad bulb, infinite.

2 TEST CONTINUITY OF THE LAMP. With a known good bulb in a socket, connect a continuity tester or multi-meter set to read resistance to both halves of the lamp's plug, as shown. Then turn the lamp switch on and off. If everything is working, the tester's lamp will blink and the meter display will shift back and forth from 0–50 to infinite ohms.

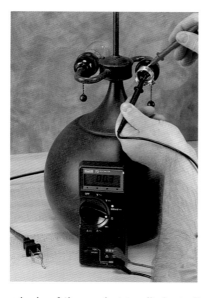

3 TEST THE CORD. A quick way to check the power cord is to connect the prongs of the lamp's plug with a piece of bare wire. Then touch the probes of a continuity tester or multi-meter to the two halves of the socket—the outer metal case and the inner metal tab, as shown. Turn the lamp's switch on and off; the tester's light should blink and the meter's display should shift between zero and infinite ohms. If they don't, press the probes to the screw terminals of the socket to eliminate the socket; the tester's light should light and a meter should display zero ohms. If not, the power cable or plug is bad.

4 TEST THE SWITCH. To test the switch, connect one probe of a multi-meter or continuity tester to one plug prong; touch the other to the socket's metal case. Turn the lamp's switch on and off. If the tester's light blinks or the meter's display shifts from zero to infinite ohms, the switch is good. If it doesn't shift, change the plug probe to the opposite probe and test again. If the display doesn't change in either position, the switch is bad.

Locating Wiring Problems

Sometimes electrical problems are caused by the wires or connections themselves. This type of problem is much trickier to locate and requires a systematic process of elimination. For situations where a fuse is blowing or a breaker is tripping, see the flowchart on page 205. This indicates that excess current is flowing because of a short circuit in a defective device (a switch, fixture, or receptacle) or in the wiring itself.

The opposite of a short is an "open," where no current flows. If you've used the procedures described earlier in this chapter and have eliminated all devices, your problem is the wiring or a bad connection. Here's where circuit mapping can come to the rescue (pages 16–19). Knowing which devices are connected to which branch circuits can drastically reduce the wiring problem possibilities.

The only way to locate bad wiring or connections is to disconnect the circuit at the service panel and check the wiring from device to device. That's why electricians are called in to troubleshoot most wiring problems. Armed with your circuit map, they'll be able to quickly and efficiently track down the problem.

Troubleshooting Flowchart

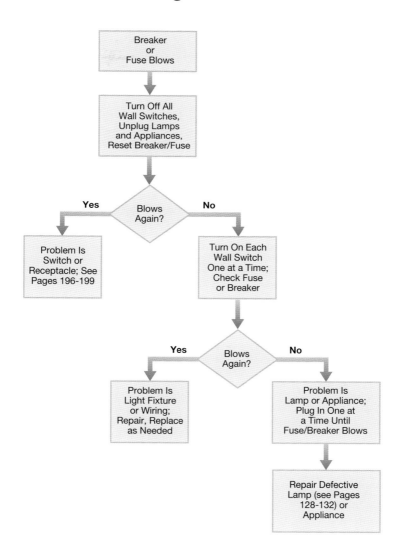

Index

A

Accent lighting, 46
Alternating current (AC), 8–9
Amp probes, 56

B

Bathroom fans, 144–151
Boxes
  installing, 72–75, 137–138
  types of, 26–30
Box extenders, 29
Box straps, 75
Branch circuits, 12–13
Breakers, 40–41, 201
Bus bars, 11

C

Cable
  ripping, 66
  routing, 67–71
  types of, 24–25
Cable lube, 96
Cable rippers, 51
Cable staplers, 160
Cable TV cable, 163–165
Can lights, 46–47, 114–119
Ceiling fans, 136–143
Ceiling medallions, 100
Circuits
  adding, 182–187
  basic, 8–9
  branch, 12–13
  extending
  surface-mounted, 170–175
  via baseboards, 176–181
  mapping, 16–19

Circuit testers, 56, 190
Combination tool, 50
Compression sleeves, 31, 65
Computer networks, 166–167
Conduit, 32–33, 90–97
Conduit benders, 52
Connections, 65–65, 76–77
Connectors
  for conduit, 90, 93
  for wire, 31
Continuity testers, 56, 190
Cover plates, 87

D

Decorative lighting, 46
Diagonal cutters, 50
Dimmer switches, 133
Direct current (DC), 8–9
Drills, electric, 53
Drywall saws, 55

E

Electrical symbols, 17
Electrical testers, 56–57, 190–193
Electrician's pliers, 51
Emergency kits, 194
Exterior low-voltage lighting,
  124–127
Eye protection, 63

F

F-connectors, 163–165
Fishing wire or cable
  with fish tape, 52, 70–71,
    184–185
  with soda straw, 162

Fuse pullers, 52
Fuses, 42, 200

G
Gangable boxes, 27
General lighting, 45
Ground-fault circuit interrupters
  (GFCI)
  described, 15, 41
  installing, 88–89
Grounding
  described, 14–15
  overhead fixtures, 102
  pigtail, 65

H
Hole saws, 116
Hot wires, 79

L
Lamps
  repairing, 128–132
  testing, 202–203
Layout tools, 54
Lighting
  installing
  exterior low-voltage, 124–127
  overhead fixtures, 100–103, 107
  recessed, 114–119
  track, 104–106
  under-cabinet, 120–123
  wall sconces, 108–113
  types of, 45–46

M
Multi-meters (multi-testers),
  56, 192

N
Needle-nose pliers, 51

O
Overhead light fixtures, 100–103,
  107

P
Parallel circuits, 9
Phone lines, 158–161

Pigtail grounds, 65. *See also*
  Grounding
Pliers, 51
Polarization, 14–15
Power distribution, 10–11
Power outages, 194–195
Push-in terminals, 77
Putty knives, 55

R
Raceway, 43, 170–175
Receptacle analyzers, 56, 191
Receptacles. *See also* Ground-
  fault circuit interrupters
  (GFCI)
  mounting, 87
  troubleshooting, 198–199
  types and grades of, 38–39
  wiring, 84–86
Recessed lighting, 46–47,
  114–119
Reciprocating saws, 53

S
Safety guidelines and equipment,
  60–61, 63
Saws, 53, 55, 116
Screwdrivers, 54
Screws, stripped, 121
Screw terminals, 76
Series circuits, 9
Service panels, 11, 44
Snakes
  described, 52
  using, 70–71, 184–185
Straws, fishing wire with, 162
Stud finders, 55
Sub-panels, 44
Surface-mounted wiring, 43,
  170–175
Switch-controlled receptacles,
  85
Switches
  installing, 133, 149–151
  mounting, 87
  troubleshooting, 196–197
  types and grades of, 34–37
  wiring, 78–83

T
Task lighting, 45
Thermostats, programmable, 152–155
Tools, types of, 50–57
Track lighting, 104–106
Troubleshooting
  breakers, 201
  electrical testers for, 56–57, 190–193
  flowchart for, 205
  fuses, 200
  lamps, 202–203
  power outages, 194–195
  receptacles, 198–199
  switches, 196–197
  wiring, 204

U
UL label, 61
Under-cabinet lighting, 120–123

Underwriter's knot, 129
Utility knives, 55

W
Wall sconces, 108–113
Wire
  cutting, 63
  joining, 64–65
  pulling through conduit, 96
  stripping, 62
  types and gauge of, 22–23
Wire nuts, 31, 64
Wire strippers, 50
Wiring
  branch circuits, 13
  connections, 76–77
  new construction, 67–71
  receptacles, 84–86
  surface-mounted, 43, 170–175
  switches, 78–83
  troubleshooting, 204

Metric Equivalency Chart
Inches to millimeters and centimeters

INCHES	MM	CM	INCHES	CM	INCHES	CM
1/8	3	0.3	9	22.9	30	76.2
1/4	6	0.6	10	25.4	31	78.7
3/8	10	1.0	11	27.9	32	81.3
1/2	13	1.3	12	30.5	33	83.8
5/8	16	1.6	13	33.0	34	86.4
3/4	19	1.9	14	35.6	35	88.9
7/8	22	2.2	15	38.1	36	91.4
1	25	2.5	16	40.6	37	94.0
1 1/4	32	3.2	17	43.2	38	96.5
1 1/2	38	3.8	18	45.7	39	99.1
1 3/4	44	4.4	19	48.3	40	101.6
2	51	5.1	20	50.8	41	104.1
2 1/2	64	6.4	21	53.3	42	106.7
3	76	7.6	22	55.9	43	109.2
3 1/2	89	8.9	23	58.4	44	111.8
4	102	10.2	24	61.0	45	114.3
4 1/2	114	11.4	25	63.5	46	116.8
5	127	12.7	26	66.0	47	119.4
6	152	15.2	27	68.6	48	121.9
7	178	17.8	28	71.1	49	124.5
8	203	20.3	29	73.7	50	127.0

mm = millimeters   cm = centimeters